RAISING TWINS

RAISING TWINS

*The Essential Guide from
Pre-birth to Young Adult*

CLARE HOUSE

In Association with

BOOKS

To Bob, Fiona, Katie and Oliver
(in alphabetical order!)

First published in Great Britain in 2011 by
JR Books, 10 Greenland Street, London NW1 0ND
www.jrbooks.com

A catalogue record for this book is available
from the British Library.

ISBN 978-1-906779-90-0

Designed by www.glensaville.com

Printed by Thomson Litho, East Kilbride

Contents

Foreword

"Congratulations! It's twins!

How did you react to those words? I remember having a surge of elation quickly followed by devastating fear. Twins? How would I cope? What would my husband say?

The next two years were a steep learning curve in man management, time management and my own character building strengths. My two gorgeous boys had no problems other than being very hungry and at their most lively in the middle of the night. They are now 17 and together we got through. This excellent book will offer you practical help and reassurance at a time when your brains are melting. You will survive !

Love Fern x"

Acknowledgements

Many people have been involved in this book in one way or another and I am extremely grateful to them all. I want to thank Emma Dally, *Prima Baby & Pregnancy Magazine* and Jeremy Robson, Ljiljana Baird and all at JR Books for helping to get *Raising Twins* started in the first place. A big thank you must go to Fern Britton for writing the foreword and to John Rush for his help. I am very grateful to Jane Donovan for all her guidance and encouraging words. I would also like to thank Carol Clay, Kate Valentine, Keith Reed and all at Tamba (the Twins and Multiple Births Association). Tamba has been an enormous help to me with all the invaluable resources it provides on its website, in all its many publications and from the very informative courses and workshops that it holds on a regular basis. My thanks too go to the Home-Start Camden team for the volunteer training I have been given and all the lovely families I have spent time with, in particular (for this book) the ones with twins. Thanks also to Kelly Andrews and the Finchley Twins Club for making me welcome at one of their meetings and to Sharon Famiglietti for letting me sit in on one of her special antenatal classes for those expecting multiples.

Very special thanks must go to my parents, Bunty and Tony George, and my parents-in-law, Bryony and Pat House, for all their wonderful grandparenting input, both for this book and for all they've done for their grandchildren. Many thanks to Diane Samuels for her inspiring writing classes, to Cath Rathbone and Richard Ehrlich for their helpful comments and encouragement, and to my son Oliver for his technical assistance. I also want to thank Fiona Dalrymple, Nicky Whiteford and Thomasina Lowe for putting me in touch with their friends with twins.

I am so grateful for the inspiring contributions from all those with twins and triplets, as well as those who are twins themselves. They have really made all the difference, so huge thanks must go to Sue Goddard, Natalie Watkins, Stephanie Modell, Jane George, Kathy Walker, Aimee Welstead, Philippa Silver, Anna Ward, Trevor and Jasmin Faulkner, Rachel Lamb, Natalia Karplus, Deborah Jackson Brown, Nicola Green, Gracieth Shimao Dias, Hilary Tulloch, Andy Astle, Sylvie Griffiths, Anna Emsley, Jessica Emsley, Lydia Emsley, and my daughters Fiona and Katie. Last but certainly not least, a big thank you to my husband Bob for a whole chapter from a father's viewpoint.

Introduction

Gemini is my star sign and as a child I always felt that there was something special about twins. However, I didn't really think about this seriously until the day I had my first scan and discovered I was pregnant with twins; it certainly opened up a whole new world for me. My mother had been told with each of her three pregnancies that she was expecting twins but back then doctors didn't have the amazing technology that they do now and relied on how many heartbeats they thought they could hear (they were all big singletons!). When I phoned to tell her the good news, she wouldn't believe me until I explained to her that I'd actually seen them on the scan. I imagine if you're reading this book the chances are that you have recently had your first scan and been given the life-changing news that two babies or more are on their way.

There is something special about being a parent of multiples. Everyone is fascinated by them. They frequently appear in literature, both classical and modern, and many cultures have their own myths surrounding them. When people discover that I am the mother of twins, they invariably ask what the experience has been like. Likewise my daughters have grown accustomed to being asked all sorts of questions. 'What's it like being a twin?' is a very common one and of course, how can they answer when it's all they know? The curiosity is always there and I'm intrigued by the interest people show.

Before the girls were born I wanted to find out as much as I could about becoming a mother of twins and was fortunate to link up with a local Twins' Club. I also joined Tamba (the Twins and Multiple Births Association). It made a big difference to be able to chat with other mothers who already had multiples and their advice was invaluable. After giving birth, I became even more aware of how different my situation was to that of most of my friends who had only one baby – having other mothers of twins to share my experiences with was a huge help.

I know that nowadays many parents find chat lines and the internet very useful and immensely helpful if you're feeling isolated and stuck at home with two or more babies. A few years ago I became a listener for Twinline, Tamba's (the Twins and Multiple Births Association) own dedicated helpline, and very quickly became aware of what an invaluable service it provides. There are times when a chat, with someone who understands what you're going through, is very reassurring. In the same way, I appreciate how my service as a volunteer with Home-Start has been of immense help to families struggling to cope with the sudden addition of two or more babies to their lives. Working alongside these families and their children under the age of five has been a very rewarding experience for me and as my own children grow up, it's been fun to still be involved with little ones. Over the years, I have been matched with quite a few families with twins and I can understand why they need additional help and support.

The suggestion to write this book came at just the right time for me. My daughters had recently left home to go to their separate universities and their departure left quite a gap in my life. Having the chance to look back over the previous twenty-one years has been therapeutic for me, as has the feeling that I can share some of my own experiences – as a mother of twins, a Twinline listener and a Home-Start volunteer working with families with twins – with those of you who are just embarking on this exciting and at times, slightly terrifying journey.

You may not have time to sit down and read *Raising Twins* all the way through right now, but I do hope that you will dip in and out of the book when you need a bit of helpful advice. I'd like to encourage you to take some time out for yourself – to sit down, put your feet up, and give yourself a few relaxing moments – it's amazing what even a 15-minute rest can do.

I have tried to cover the main questions that you may be asking at each of the different stages of growing up that your children will go through. I've been fortunate to have been in touch with a number of other parents of twins who have kindly allowed me to quote from their own experiences and I hope you will find their anecdotes helpful and reassuring. Raising twins is by no means an easy task and we all have good and bad days but I think when you look back on it all, you will definitely agree that the good times far outweigh anything else. There really is something very special about having twins, triplets or even more and I hope there will be times when you feel truly blessed. As one mother whose children had recently started at secondary school said:

'I think the great thing about having multiples is the fun they have together – they are never short of a playmate and there is much fun and laughter in the house. Surprisingly, they don't really fight much (at the moment anyway!). Everyone says that having multiples must be really hard work – and it was when they were young – but now they are older, we reap the rewards!'

Chapter 1

Pregnancy

'Imagine my surprise
when what I thought was
indigestion turned out
to be the fact that I was
expecting twins.'

Today couples are better prepared for the fact that they are having twins (or more). The babies make their first appearance in your initial scan at around twelve weeks. Nevertheless, there is still the surprise element when you go in for the scan and discover that you are expecting more than one baby. I still remember the feeling I had when I travelled back to work on the Underground with my life changing news. 'No one on this train knows but me – I'm expecting twins!' It's an exciting and for some new mothers an overwhelming realisation that a whole new world awaits them not of one baby but two!

'I managed to miss my bus stop – I was that shocked, having just had my first scan which revealed I was expecting twins!'

'My very first words were, 'Why me?' and then I burst into tears and kept repeating them. My husband said, 'Wow!' and laughed and then in reply to my 'Why Me?' he said, 'Because we are part of an elite group and can handle this, no problem. Can't wait!'

'My reaction was one of joy: I was pleased. My partner's reaction was probably shock. He wasn't with me when I had the scan (my mother was). I phoned him to tell him the news and asked him to sit down.'

The most recent statistics produced by Tamba (www.tamba.org.uk) indicate a woman has a one in ninety chance of giving birth to twins. You are far more likely to have twins if they run in the family on the maternal side and four times more likely if you already have fraternal twins. Having said that, identical twins are not hereditary, they are 'a fluke of nature'. You are also more likely to have twins if you're in your late thirties when you become pregnant or if you already have a large family. In the last thirty years multiple births have increased as a result of IVF (in vitro fertilisation) as well. One in four IVF births results in twins while one in twenty-two IVF births are triplets.

'We both found the whole IVF scenario absolutely fine. I suffered no side effects from it and apart from the initial endless scans and blood tests, it was totally non-intrusive and I would recommend it to anyone.'

Approximately one third of all twins are monozygotic (identical). This is when the egg splits after it has been fertilised to produce identical babies. Identical twins have the same genes, the same physical features and are the same sex. Non-identical (dizygotic or fraternal twins) are conceived when you produce two eggs and they are each fertilised by a different sperm during the same menstrual cycle. There are even cases of fraternal twins having different fathers. Conjoined (Siamese) twins are always identical and an extremely rare occurrence when the egg splits after around twelve to fifteen days.

Your First Scan

The first scan determines how many babies you are having and whether or not they are in the same amniotic sac. At this stage, you will also be checked to see if there is more than one placenta. If the babies share one placenta there is a small chance that they may be affected by Twin to Twin Transfusion Syndrome (TTTS). This is when blood from one baby is transferred to the other and it can have serious consequences.

Separate/Shared placentas

There are three possible twin formations which your scan can show. These are:

- Monochorionic Diamniotic (MCDA) twins share a placenta and an outer membrane but each has its own amniotic sac. These babies will be identical.

- Monochorionic Monoamniotic (MCMA) twins are extremely rare. They share a placenta, an outer membrane and a single amniotic sac. Only about 1 per cent of Monochorionic twins are MCMA. These babies will be identical. Because they are both in the same sac there is a risk of cord entanglement which can hinder the babies' movement. For this reason, such twins are usually delivered by Caesarean.
- Dichorionic Diamniotic (DCDA) twins each have their own placenta and amniotic sac but share an outer membrane. About two-thirds of DCDA twins are non-identical and one-third are identical. In some cases, the two placentas can fuse during pregnancy.

MCDA and MCMA twins are at risk of TTTS – statistics show that it can affect between 10 and 15 per cent of monochorionic twins.DCDA twins are not at risk of TTTS.

Ask for the picture of your babies after you've had the first scan – it will help you to believe it's happening. It is usually possible to get a copy of the scan to take home but some hospitals may charge for this.

Between eighteen and twenty-four weeks your hospital may carry out an anomaly scan to check on the babies' development and the position of the placenta(s). From twenty-four weeks onwards it is likely that you will have more regular scans. This depends on the hospital, whether or not the babies share a placenta and if there is any other reason why the hospital feels you may need to be more regularly monitored. It might seem like an imposition at the time but it is definitely in the interest of you and your babies that these scans are carried out. At around thirty-four weeks the scan will show the position the babies are likely to be in at the time of delivery and this determines whether or not you will need to have a Caesarean (C-section). You may find that your hospital policy dictates you must have a Caesarean if you are having multiple babies.

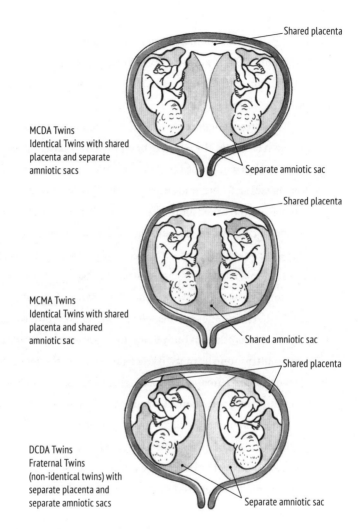

MCDA Twins
Identical Twins with shared
placenta and separate
amniotic sacs

Shared placenta

Separate amniotic sac

MCMA Twins
Identical Twins with shared
placenta and shared
amniotic sac

Shared placenta

Shared amniotic sac

DCDA Twins
Fraternal Twins
(non-identical twins) with
separate placenta and
separate amniotic sacs

Shared placenta

Separate amniotic sac

Additional Tests

There are other tests that you will be offered by your antenatal team.
One of these is the nuchal translucency (NT scan), which checks
for Down's syndrome. This is takes place within the first trimester
(three months) and involves measuring the thickness of the babies'
necks. There is no risk to the unborn children. This test only tells
you each baby's chances of having Down's syndrome. The chances

are high if the results are one in fifty and low if they are one in 5,000. If the nuchal translucency scan shows your chances are high, you will be offered further tests to determine whether either baby has Down's syndrome.

These tests are known as the amniocentesis test (amniotic fluid test or AFT) and the CVS (Chorionic Villus Sampling). In both cases an invasive procedure is necessary. Amniocentesis is usually done between fifteen and twenty weeks. Using a fine needle for each baby, a sample of amniotic fluid is taken from the placenta(s) and the foetal cells are identified. The CVS also gives information on a baby's chromosomes but in this test samples are taken directly from the chorionic villi (fragments of placenta) using a needle through the abdomen, or in some cases via the cervix with a fine tube or forceps. The CVS test is done between eleven and thirteen weeks so you will get an earlier result. In both cases, local anaesthetic is administered and an ultrasound scan used to ensure neither the foetuses nor the placenta(s) are damaged. Because these tests are more complicated when multiple pregnancies are involved, you may be required to have them done at a specialist hospital. There is a small risk of foetal injury or miscarriage so you should ask the hospital to advise you on the risks involved before you make the decision to go ahead. It is also a good idea to discuss the risks with your partner before making any decisions.

Taking Care of Yourself

What to Eat

One of the early signs of pregnancy is an increased appetite but it is not advisable to eat for three (or four or even more!). When you are expecting twins, it is suggested you need about one and a half times the daily calories that you would require if expecting one baby, which means approximately 600 extra calories per day. Your GP/midwife can give you helpful guidelines on what to eat for a healthy pregnancy but it is worth noting that you need more protein, calcium, iron, folic acid and vitamin B12 than in a singleton pregnancy. Good sources of protein are chicken, lean meat, fish, cheese, eggs and pulses. Iron is found in red meat, wholemeal bread, pulses (such as beans and lentils), dark green vegetables and fortified breakfast cereals. A healthy, well-balanced diet is always recommended and many health professionals suggest you take iron and vitamin supplements (it is always worth checking with your GP or midwife first).

You may find that eating little and often is what suits you best. It's a good idea to have healthy snacks with you when you're out and about to keep energy levels up – these could include dried fruit, cereal bars, bananas or flapjacks. You may also find it helpful to have a few light and easily digestible snacks beside your bed in case you wake up in the night feeling hungry.

What Not to Eat

During pregnancy it is advisable not to eat soft cheeses, blue cheeses or any kind of pâté. Raw eggs, unpasteurised milk and raw meat must be avoided as they may contain salmonella. You are also advised not to eat more than two portions of oily fish a week as they could contain harmful pollutants. Caffeine can be harmful to your babies, so avoid if possible drinking tea, coffee, colas or high-energy drinks. Similarly drinking alcohol during pregnancy carries a risk to the unborn babies. Fortunately there is a high incidence of pregnant women who lose their taste for alcohol. In fact, because of a heightened sense of smell that develops during pregnancy you may find you lose your taste for certain foods and other drinks as well.

Foods Recommended To Add to Your Diet

- Nuts which are high in protein. Almonds are good for vitamin E and cashews are particularly rich in minerals.
- Unsweetened breakfast cereals which have been fortified with vitamins, iron and folic acid will provide a good healthy snack between meals as well as giving you a good start to the day. Some are high in fibre too which has the added benefit of helping your digestive system.
- Yoghurt is rich in calcium as well as being a good source of protein. It's better to avoid yoghurts which have added sugar. Instead make your own concoction with plain yoghurt and add fresh or dried fruits, nuts, cereals and honey.
- Hummus, which is made from chickpeas, is a good source of protein, fibre and folic acid and can be added to sandwiches or used as a dip for chopped fresh vegetables.
- Eggs are high in protein and make a quick easy snack when hard boiled. They can also be added to salads.
- Spinach is very good for calcium, folic acid, iron, fibre and vitamins K and C. Add raw to your salads or cook.
- Peanut butter is also a good source for protein and contains beneficial minerals such as potassium and zinc.
- As you get bigger you may well find that you lose your appetite but it is still important to feed yourself and your babies well. You may find that you'd rather make a healthy smoothie if you're not feeling particularly hungry. Add yoghurt to provide that extra bit of calcium and protein.

Exercise

Gentle exercise such as swimming and walking is good for you during pregnancy and it is definitely advisable to practise pelvic floor exercises too. Swimming is an excellent form of non-weight bearing exercise which will not disturb the babies. In addition, water has the added benefit of making you feel weightless – not something you will experience all that often when pregnant, let alone with twins.

Yoga during pregnancy has become very popular and can be practised when you are expecting twins (there are special antenatal yoga classes particularly geared towards pregnant women). Pilates is another form of exercise that is ideal during pregnancy as it is gentle and low-impact but at the same time helps you to strengthen your abdominal, pelvic floor and back muscles.

If you've never been to a yoga or pilates class find one that is dedicated to pregnant mums. As well as keeping you fit and flexible, they are good for teaching you how to relax. You must be more conscious of what your body is going through when pregnant, however, so don't over-do it and always make sure you get plenty of rest as well. If there is not a specialist teacher in your area contact your nearest fitness centre who may be able to advise you. As you get bigger, you will feel the need to slow down and you'll have every excuse for taking a well-earned afternoon nap.

DO NOT participate in sports that involve any danger of falling – ski-ing, horse riding, cycling, gymnastics and ball sports – where there is any risk of being hit in the stomach.

‘During my pregnancy I started going to a yoga class for pregnant mums. I found it very helpful but I did find that there were some exercises I couldn't manage just because I was so much bigger than the other mums there!’

Rest

With all the changes that your body will be going through you will feel particularly tired in the first few weeks of pregnancy. You may find that you are sleeping longer than usual and if you can get between 8 to 10 hours of sleep each night you will welcome this. As you get bigger, it won't be so easy to stay in bed for long stretches without feeling uncomfortable, so if possible try to have a nap, or at least put aside some time when you can take things easy during the day. If you are able to lie down that's ideal, but if not find a comfortable chair to relax in with your feet up and read or listen to soothing music and give yourself a chance to recharge your batteries. It's important to do some exercise each day, but as you get bigger you may not feel up to doing much. Listen to your body – it's important that you don't overdo things. During the latter stages of your pregnancy try to take an afternoon nap whenever possible as you will be very big and your body will need the rest.

Lying down

It's not recommended that you lie on your back when sleeping as your womb will be pressing on major blood vessels and this can make you light headed. The best position is to lie on your left side as this promotes optimal blood flow to your body and uterus. You can support your tummy with a pillow and place another between your knees, or you might want to consider a body pillow for extra comfort. You can also support your back with a pillow; this will stop you rolling onto your back too. You may find that, as you become larger, you are more comfortable in a semi-reclined position; you can achieve this by propping yourself up on pillows.

If you're finding it difficult to get to sleep you could try having a warm bath or shower just before bedtime to help you to feel more relaxed. Avoid having any caffeinated drinks in the evenings – try a soothing camomile tea instead.

What to wear

It is likely that you will need to start looking at maternity clothes sooner than you would if you were expecting one baby, but it is possible to stay in your favourite clothes for a little longer if you get yourself a belly belt and a belly band. A belly belt attaches to your trouser fastenings and allows you quite a bit of growing space, making them more comfortable to wear as your tummy gets bigger. A belly band covers your bump and will hide any unfastened buttons or the fact that your favourite top is not quite long enough. It's also useful to cover your midriff when breastfeeding.

Rather than buying a lot of maternity clothes you may want to consider getting fewer items of a better quality that you are more likely to want to wear regularly. Maternity tights and good maternity bras are definitely worth buying and leggings are always useful.

You might want to treat yourself to a nice maternity nightie or pyjamas as the chances are you may be in hospital for a few days and family and friends will be coming to visit you there and at home. You may not feel up to getting properly dressed when you first come home too. If you know you're going to have a Caesarean you'll want to have some comfortable clothes to wear afterwards – loose jogging bottoms are always popular.

No Smoking

It is commonly known that smoking during pregnancy reduces the oxygen supply to babies and increases the already high risk of them being born early and underweight so it's just not worth it.

Medications

You should always check with your GP/midwife about any medication you may be taking – even over-the-counter medication can be harmful to you and your babies during pregnancy.

Pampering yourself

Once your babies are here you're really not going to get much time for yourself so try to give yourself a few treats whilst you can. Even if you're only taking 10 or 20 minutes a day to do something just for you this will help to relax you, to relieve stress and this is certainly good for you and for your babies. Think of things that you're unlikely to be able to do for some time once your babies are born.

Pampering Tips

- Giving your feet a good soak in warm water with lavender oil
- Having a warm bath by candlelight
- Getting a haircut
- Sitting comfortably and reading a good book
- Having a reflexology session
- Enjoying a massage with someone experienced in massage during pregnancy
- Going to see a film with a few girlfriends
- Going out to dinner with your husband/partner
- Having a lie-in in the morning
- Or doing absolutely nothing at all! That in itself may be a treat

Essential Oils

You should also be aware that using certain essential oils such as those used in aromatherapy can be harmful during pregnancy. Do not use nutmeg, rosemary, basil, jasmine, clary sage, sage and juniper berry. Aromatherapy has been known to help with backache, nausea or swollen ankles but you should always consult your midwife first. It is particularly advisable not to use essential oils during the first trimester. Always consult an aromatherapist who is qualified to treat pregnant women: The Institute for Complementary Medicine (www.i-c-m.org.uk) will be able to advise you on this.

Travel

As your pregnancy progresses and your bump gets bigger you may find that travelling on public transport becomes more difficult. This is particularly the case if you have to travel during rush hour, but there are seats specially designated for people like you and you should make use of them. If no one makes a move to offer a seat to you (and they should when they see your bump coming!) do ask as generally people are only too happy to give up their seat. If you can avoid travelling at busy times it will be a lot easier for you.

When travelling by car ensure that you wear a three-point seat belt above and below your bump and not over it. As you will feel more tired during your pregnancy it is not a good idea to drive on your own on long journeys. Try to share the driving with someone else and make sure that you stop regularly to give yourself a break and a chance to stretch your legs.

If you are planning on going abroad on holiday it is worth thinking of doing this after the first twelve weeks when you won't be feeling quite so tired and hopefully won't be experiencing morning sickness. If you are travelling by air or ferry you will need to check each operator's policy on travel for pregnant women before making your bookings. It's important that they know you are expecting multiples as their policies may be different. You should also consult your doctor or midwife to ensure that they are happy for you to go and ask for written permission from them just in case you should be asked for it. As you are likely to look more pregnant than you are because you're carrying two or more babies it's important to make certain that you're not going to run into any difficulties.

You will also need to check what travel insurance cover you have and check that you're travelling somewhere where the medical facilities are appropriate. It's best to avoid travelling to countries that require you to have immunisations and/or take anti-malaria tablets as these are not advisable during pregnancy. Check whether it's safe to drink the tap water and if it isn't buy bottled water.

If travelling by air on a long flight make sure you drink plenty of water to keep hydrated and get up and move around the aircraft regularly. There is a small risk of deep vein thrombosis (DVT) so you may want to consider wearing special flight socks but do make sure they fit properly. You shouldn't fly in small planes that don't have pressurised cabins.

Antenatal Classes

Antenatal classes are designed to prepare you for the birth of your babies. They usually cover what to expect during your pregnancy and how to keep yourself and your babies healthy. You will be taught about the different stages of labour, what pain relief is all about and some useful relaxation techniques. Your health after giving birth, looking after your babies, breastfeeding and bottle feeding are also topics that are likely to be covered. Classes are usually held once a week and are generally in blocks of ten. Some classes are just for pregnant women and some are for husbands/partners too. You should have the chance to ask any questions you might have during your antenatal classes.

It is far more common for twins to be born early – the average twin pregnancy is thirty-seven weeks. So, if you are working, it may be a good idea to stop at around twenty-eight weeks. By this stage you will be feeling more tired, you'll also be getting very big and will definitely find yourself in need of more rest.

It is a good idea to book in early for antenatal classes ... otherwise you may not complete the course! Try and start between twenty and twenty-four weeks so that you can attend all the sessions before your babies are born. Antenatal classes are also a good way to meet other parents expecting at the same time as you and who live in your area.

There are now antenatal sessions specifically designed to prepare you for a multiple birth (contact www.tamba.org.uk for further information) and the Multiple Births Foundation organises meetings at Queen Charlotte's & Chelsea Hospital in West London.

Tamba conducted a survey in 2008 which revealed that only 33 per cent of women pregnant with multiples were offered multiple-specific antenatal classes. It can also be the case that if you have already had a child prior to having multiples, you may not be offered any type of antenatal class.

‘I wasn't offered antenatal classes at all but felt this was due to the fact I had already had a child. It would have been good to have been offered a twins' course, though!’

Maternity Leave

As long as all is going well with your pregnancy and your job doesn't involve doing anything too strenuous or stressful, you should be able to continue working. Bear in mind that with multiples, you are likely to go into labour earlier so if possible, try to give yourself a few weeks of rest before your babies are born. You could look at finishing work around twenty-eight weeks. As you get bigger, you may be able to work from home or at least change your hours slightly so that you're not having to travel during rush-hour times. Make sure you talk this over with your employers in good time so that you're all in agreement.

Unfortunately having multiples does not entitle you to longer maternity leave or to more maternity pay. You can take a year's maternity leave with nine months' pay. The amount you are paid will depend on how long you have worked for your current employer, whether your job is full- or part-time and your salary at the time. You may either qualify for Statutory Maternity Pay (SMP) or Maternity Allowance (MA). Rules are constantly changing, so check this with your employer but you can also get detailed information from the Department for Work and Pensions at www.dwp.gov.uk.

While on maternity leave, you can still stay in contact with your company. You might suggest that they keep you up to date by email or you can catch up with colleagues so that you are up to speed with what's going on.

‘My pregnancy started out OK but once I got to twenty-six weeks I began feeling uncomfortable and very restless. I was pleased that I wasn't working.’

‘*At week thirty-two I was still working full time (definitely a mistake).*’

Those who have been able to attend multi-specific antenatal classes have found them extremely helpful. As a result, Tamba now offers special antenatal classes for those expecting twins or more and these are proving to be enormously popular. They are currently run as an intensive one-day course for six couples and focus on all aspects of labour, birth, breastfeeding and many other issues that particularly concern parents expecting multiples. These multiple-specific classes are held at least once a month in different venues around the country and Tamba is increasing the number to meet the rising demand.

Since these classes are proving so popular it is a good idea to book in plenty of time and bear in mind that they are aimed at those who are twenty-plus weeks pregnant. Attendees have found them extremely helpful, not only for gaining knowledge and information but also for meeting others expecting multiples.

'I found my local antenatal classes helpful but the special one organised for those expecting multiples made all the difference. It was reassuring to be with a group of people who were in the same boat as us.'

It is definitely worth going to the classes offered by your hospital as well, even if they're not for multiples, as it is helpful for you to get to know the midwives and other staff at the hospital, to have a tour of the place and to meet other families who will have children of a similar age to yours and live locally. It is also important that you ask to be shown the Neonatal Intensive Care Unit (NICU), also known as the Special Care Baby Unit (SCBU). It is much more likely that one or both of your babies may spend a bit of time there and if you're not able to go there after the birth, at least you know exactly where they will be and whose capable hands will be responsible for their well-being

The Multiple Births Foundation (www.multiplebirthsfoundation. org.uk) organise a 'Preparing for Twins and Triplets' evening at Queen Charlotte's & Chelsea Hospital in Hammersmith, West London. These evenings are generally held once a month from 7.30– 9.30 p.m. and begin with an illustrated talk by the MBF, followed by question time with a local Twins' Club. If you don't live too far from London, it is well worth booking to attend. Otherwise the MBF website contains some helpful information on having twins or higher multiples.

The National Childbirth Trust (NCT) also offer antenatal classes but generally these are not multiple-specific.

Twins' Clubs

There are a large number of local Twins' Clubs all over the country. To find the one nearest to you, visit the Tamba website or contact them directly. It's a good idea to get in touch with your local Twins' Club before your babies are born; that way you can find out in advance where and how often they meet, whether they hold secondhand sales and any local tips they can offer you. If you have the chance to pop in to one of their drop-ins before the birth, you may find that the other members can give you helpful advice. There will be several mother (parent/carer) and baby groups in your area which are always useful and it can be reassuring to meet up with others who, like you, have more than one baby.

Your midwife may be able to tell you whether there are other mothers-to-be in your area who are also expecting multiples, or who already have young twins or more. It makes a big difference to know that you're going through the same thing together.

Before You Give Birth

It is a good idea to find out early in your pregnancy what your local health authority's procedures are for women expecting twins or more. Ask how often you will be expected to attend appointments and what antenatal tests you will be offered. It may be that your hospital provides antenatal classes specifically for those who are pregnant with twins or more. Before going for check-ups, make a list of any questions you may have – it's very easy to forget them once you're there. They say that women become more forgetful when pregnant and it's generally true! Discuss any concerns you may have, however trivial they might seem to you: it's important that you have things clear in your mind.

Antenatal Care

To begin with, your antenatal care is likely be similar to that of any mother expecting but as time progresses, you will probably have more check-ups, more scans and your babies may need to be monitored more regularly. You will also have your blood pressure measured more frequently and more blood and urine tests will be done. There is no fixed rule as to how you will be looked after – this varies from place to place and it is always a good idea to check with your local health centre as to how they deal with twin pregnancies so you know what to expect. In some areas the midwife handles the antenatal care and in others it is all done through a GP or your local hospital. Hospitals usually organise a visit to the labour ward as part of their antenatal classes and it is a good idea to familiarise yourself with the hospital layout.

‛One piece of advice I was very glad I was given was to visit the neonatal unit in the hospital before my babies were born. As it happened, one of them needed a bit of help with her breathing and spent her first three days in the unit.’

With twins and other multiple births it is more than likely that at least one of your babies may have to spend some time in the neo-natal unit and you might not be in a position to see them straightaway. You will feel much more reassured knowing where they are and that they are in competent hands.

Bed Rest in Hospital Due to High Blood Pressure

'I was admitted to hospital when I was about thirty-two weeks due to high blood pressure and had to stay in for two or three days. As it was a teaching hospital, I did become the focus of attention for medical students. One funny thing happened when the obstetrician came in on his own asking if he could bring a group of students to see me. Would I mind if they each had the chance to feel my pregnant tummy? But he didn't want me to reveal that I was expecting twins. Having got used to being poked and prodded about by now and feeling a bit bored and lonely in the room I had been given to myself, I agreed.

'In they came and the obstetrician asked them to ascertain what position the baby was in. They all had a good feel and confidently pronounced their different opinions. Yes, they could definitely feel the baby's head here. No, said another, the baby's head is definitely here – but not one of them suspected for a minute that there might have been more than one baby! It was worth it all for the look on their faces when the obstetrician asked me to tell them the correct position and I pointed out that at that time one of my daughters was in the breech position and the other was lying in the transverse position!'

Changes to Your Body

During pregnancy the female body goes through all kinds of changes and when you are expecting two or more babies, you are likely to feel these changes even more. You will probably be extremely tired to begin with and you may find your appetite increases. There will be some foods that you crave and others you totally reject. Your breasts will most likely feel particularly tender and it is a good idea to wear a properly fitted bra during this time. With extra pressure on your bladder, you will need to urinate more frequently. Understandably you are likely to be a lot bigger sooner and may find you need to wear loose-fitting clothing from an early stage. Because you are likely to get very big, it is worth thinking ahead when buying (or borrowing) clothes. Where possible, try to choose clothes that will grow with you.

'As my bump got so big, I was able to use it like a lap tray and could eat my dinner from it – it was *that* big!'

Side Effects

The following are some of the side effects that accompany pregnancy and which you are more likely to experience because you are carrying two or more babies.

Morning Sickness

Not everyone gets it, but some mothers have commented that their morning sickness was far worse when expecting twins than when they were pregnant with just one baby.

'For the first twenty-two weeks I suffered with morning sickness – I'm glad it didn't last any longer.'

I suffered from morning sickness which started with queasy feelings at nine weeks and by week ten, was sick every day during the morning and it finally subsided the day I gave birth!

Your Sex Life

Not everyone feels like having sex during pregnancy, particularly once your bump starts getting bigger, but as long as you have no complications or have been specifically advised not to have sex, there is no problem with getting intimate with your partner. What you might find harder is actually doing it, but with a bit of imagination you'll succeed! The 'Spoons' position where you lay on your side and your partner lies behind you is good for closeness and avoids pressure on your tummy. Try to organise some special time together before your babies are born – you will not get much chance for some time afterwards.

You or your partner may be worried that your babies could be at risk during sexual intercourse but the thick mucus plug that seals the cervix during this time keeps them protected from infection. They are also protected by the amniotic sac(s) and your strong uterus muscles. The exceptions to this are if you have a history of cervical weakness or premature labour or if you have a low-lying placenta(s). If in doubt, always consult your GP or midwife.

You can feel nauseous at any time but particularly if you haven't eaten for a while and that's why morning sickness is more common in the morning. Eating small amounts often helps and certain foods will help to ease it. Ginger seems to do the trick for some; try a ginger herbal tea or a gingernut biscuit, or some freshly grated ginger on your salad or added to a noodle dish. Meat, fish, eggs and dairy products eaten in small quantities can help also. Morning sickness usually passes after the first three months but unfortunately some women experience it throughout their entire pregnancy. Consult your GP or midwife if you are being sick often as this can lead to dehydration and low blood pressure.

Constipation

Unfortunately this is a common problem in multiple pregnancies and constipation can lead to piles (haemorrhoids). It is caused partly by pressure from your growing uterus on the rectum and so if you're carrying two or more babies, it is more likely to happen. Additionally, the hormones your body produces during pregnancy slow down bowel action. Eating foods with plenty of fibre content will help. Good sources of foods high in fibre include breakfast cereals such as porridge oats, wholemeal bread, brown rice, pulses, fruit and vegetables. It is recommended you drink six to eight glasses of water each day too. Prunes and prune juice, dried apricots (contain sorbitol which stimulates the bowel) are also known to help prevent constipation.

If you're not used to eating food with a high fibre content, start off gradually, or you could feel a bit bloated at first. Go to the toilet as soon as you need to. Some iron tablets can make constipation worse so your midwife or GP may recommend an alternative. Always consult them first before buying over-the-counter remedies. Gentle exercise such as swimming, walking or yoga can be helpful.

Piles (Haemmorrhoids)

With your growing babies pressing down inside you, blood flow can become obstructed and cause dilated veins in the area of your anus. These may become itchy or sore but are not dangerous. During bowel movements, however, they can bleed and may be made worse if you become constipated so make sure you eat sufficient fibre-filled foods and drink lots of water. Taking regular exercise, even if it's just going for a walk every day can help, too. Avoid straining when you do go to the toilet. It is best to go when you need to rather than making yourself wait. You will find that using soft toilet paper or wet wipes makes it less painful. There are over-the-counter remedies for piles but it is best to check with your GP or pharmacist first before using them.

Varicose Veins

It is common for the veins in your legs to become swollen during pregnancy (particularly with a multiple pregnancy) and sometimes they can become quite painful. Your GP may prescribe special pregnancy support tights and socks to help. It is a good idea to wear shoes with a small heel rather than totally flat shoes or high heels. When sitting, try putting your feet up (you have the perfect excuse!) and avoid standing for long periods. If you have to stand for any length of time, keep moving your legs and where possible, go for a walk to keep the blood flowing. While it is still comfortable to lie on your back, stretch out on the floor with your feet up against the wall to ease the pressure you feel in your legs. Get up slowly afterwards.

Cramps

During the second and third trimesters of your pregnancy you may find yourself waking up with painful leg cramps. They can be caused by a shortage of essential nutrients and salts such as calcium or magnesium getting to your blood as your babies are taking them all. It's uncertain whether supplements help with cramps but you should always check with your GP first.

If you do get cramps, you need to massage and stretch the muscle. At first, it will be painful but if you straighten your leg, heel first and then stretch the ankles and toes, you will gradually feel better.

Doing calf stretches, particularly just before bedtime, may also help. Foot exercises where you bend and stretch each foot up and down thirty times a day and rotate eight times in each direction can alleviate the problem. Try a warm bath before bed and lie on your left side to improve circulation to and from your legs. If the cramps persist, however, do consult your midwife or GP.

Backache

It is common to experience lower back pain during pregnancy, particularly if you're expecting more than one baby. The extra weight you are carrying puts a strain on the spine and as your tummy muscles are more stretched than normal, they cannot do their usual job of stabilising your back. Also, the hormone relaxin (which softens and stretches the ligaments in preparation for labour) makes it more likely for you to feel a greater number of aches and pains. Be aware of maintaining a good posture and wear flatter shoes. If you need to bend down to pick something up, make sure you bend at the knees or go down on one knee rather than curving your back round. As your pregnancy develops, you won't be able to bend over easily anyway but it is good to put this into practice right from the beginning.

Try not to pick up anything heavy; this is particularly difficult if you already have a small child/toddler but you must look after yourself. When getting out of bed, you will find it easier to roll over onto your side first especially during the latter part of your pregnancy, then put your feet on the floor before sitting up. Even simple everyday tasks such as getting out of bed can become quite a challenge.

Regular exercise such as swimming, yoga and pilates also helps to reduce backache. Massage can alleviate it and you may find that sleeping on your side with a pillow under your tummy helps too. Do talk to your GP about using a support belt to help carry the weight of your babies.

Tips for Heartburn

- Avoid foods that are spicy, tomato and tomato based products overly fatty, hot sauces and condiments.
- Avoid caffeine and carbonated beverages that can also contribute to heartburn.
- Eat several small meals during the day instead of three large ones.
- Have your last meal of the day at least one hour before going to bed.
- Add milk and especially yoghurt to your daily diet as they can also help neutralise your stomach acid.
- Avoid drinking lots of fluids during meals as this can distend your stomach.
- Try chewing some gum after meals; this also helps neutralise stomach acids.
- If you can, sleep propped up with extra pillows so your head is higher than your stomach.
- Make sure your clothes aren't too tight.
- Do some gentle yoga-type exercises. Some women have found that stretching their arms above their heads to elongate the upper body eases heartburn.
- Try going for a gentle walk after eating to aid your digestion.
- Remedies such as Gaviscon can make a difference and are free on prescription from your GP. Always check with your pharmacist or GP first before taking over-the-counter remedies.

Heartburn and Indigestion

During pregnancy your body produces more progesterone, the primary hormone produced by your body during pregnancy. One side effect of this is that the muscles to the entrance of your stomach can become more relaxed and this allows stomach acid to flow back up, causing heartburn or indigestion. This is exacerbated by your enlarged uterus pressing on your stomach, which also causes stomach acid to flow up into your oesophagus and to give a burning sensation.

Tiredness and Insomnia

Feeling very tired is another early indication of pregnancy and wherever possible, you should try and rest more to help your body cope with the changes it's going through. As your pregnancy progresses and you become larger, it is not so easy to sleep comfortably through the night. I always feel that interrupted sleep during pregnancy (particularly in the latter stages) is nature's way of preparing you for what's to come!

‘Then from thirty weeks came the sleepless nights and difficulties in climbing stairs. I was very tired by 8 p.m. and only just managed to last to around 9.30 most evenings.’

Try and make yourself as comfortable as you can – if necessary with the help of extra pillows. Rather than lying on your back, lie on your side and support your tummy with a pillow. Avoid drinking tea or coffee in the evening and try not to drink anything about an hour before you go to bed to avoid having to get up in the night. Your babies may well decide to become extra-active the moment you lie down to rest. Stroke your tummy, enjoy the contact and hopefully they won't keep you awake for too long!

Swollen Feet and Hands

During the later stages of your pregnancy, particularly when the weather is hot, you may experience mild swelling of the feet. This is not uncommon but it is a good idea to mention it to your GP or midwife as it could indicate pre-eclampsia (a condition that causes high blood pressure in pregnant women). Around this time of your pregnancy, there is more fluid and blood circulating through your body and because of gravity, some of this additional fluid will remain in your feet causing the swelling.

At this point, wear comfortable shoes, avoid tight-fitting socks or tights and put your feet up whenever you can. Try not to spend too much time standing. Gentle exercise helps to disperse the fluids that have settled in your feet and so walking can help, as can aqua aerobics. Sometimes your hands may also become swollen and if this is the case, it's a good idea to remove any rings.

‘As I got bigger and the weather got hotter, I definitely began to feel like a beached whale!’

‘*From twenty-eight weeks my legs, hands and arms became swollen, particularly my ankles, and I felt like I was sloshing when I walked. I called it "dead-leg syndrome" but a daily foot and leg massage from my gorgeous hubby helped out no end!*’

Stretch Marks

Not everyone is left with stretch marks after a twin pregnancy. During the last couple of months you may find your skin becomes itchy on your back and lower abdomen; it is believed that as your skin stretches it becomes drier. Try not to scratch, as aggravating it will release histamines which makes the skin even itchier. Moisturise, Moisturise, Moisturise! You can use bath oils and body lotions (preferably unperfumed); some women find that Vitamin E cream helps. Avoid excessively hot water when showering and bathing. If you find that the itching becomes unbearable and spreads to other areas of your body contact your GP as this could be an indication of obstetric cholestasis.

Pelvic Girdle Pain

Throughout pregnancy your body produces the hormone relaxin and during a multiple pregnancy, the body produces even more. This causes the ligaments holding the bones in your pelvis to loosen and with the extra weight carried, you may become extremely uncomfortable and experience considerable pain. If this happens to you, do let your GP or midwife know. They may refer you to an obstetric physiotherapist, who will advise on the correct posture to adopt, give you special exercises to strengthen the area and suggest you wear a support girdle for comfort.

Carpal Tunnel Syndrome (CTS)

If you find that your wrists feel swollen and you experience a tingling sensation rather like pins and needles in your fingers during pregnancy it is possible that you may have carpal tunnel syndrome. This is caused by the extra fluid you are carrying putting pressure on the nerve channel in your wrist. It can also make your hands feel numb and much weaker, and in the worst cases cause considerable pain in your hands and in your arms too. You may notice that it gets worse at night. Sleeping with your hands raised on a pillow reduces the amount of fluid built up during the day. Gently exercising your hands and fingers and stretching them above your head can also help to ease the discomfort. If it continues to bother you, do consult your GP or midwife.

Complications during Pregnancy

It is worth being aware of the complications that can occur during a multiple pregnancy but at the same time please bear in mind that they rarely occur. Regular antenatal appointments should be kept as these are designed to ensure that you do not suffer any form of complication. However, if you do have concerns, it is always best to talk them through with your GP or midwife just in case.

Anaemia

Most pregnant women will experience a mild form of anaemia but if you are expecting twins or more, then the chances of developing this are even higher. Your babies will be absorbing more nutrients from your blood and this can cause increased tiredness, shortness of breath and sometimes even fainting. One of the many routine blood tests that you will have during pregnancy indicates whether you are anaemic and if you are, you may be recommended iron supplements to counteract this. Add iron-rich foods such as green vegetables, red meat, beans and lentils to your daily diet to help you avoid becoming anaemic.

Pre-Eclampsia

You should be aware that the likelihood of pre-eclampsia occurring is greater during a twin pregnancy. A survey carried out by Tamba in 2008 showed that 16 per cent of mothers expecting twins or triplets experienced pre-eclampsia. The signs are raised blood pressure, swelling of the ankles, legs and fingers and/or protein in your urine. Throughout your pregnancy, your blood pressure is regularly monitored and you will be asked to give a urine sample at your antenatal appointments to check for irregular levels of protein. If you have any concerns, contact your midwife or GP immediately. If you do develop pre-eclampsia, it is highly likely you will be admitted to hospital for bed rest, where you will be closely monitored.

Gestational Diabetes

Gestational diabetes is diagnosed when raised blood sugar levels are detected during pregnancy. It is routinely checked for when you give urine samples. Symptoms of gestational diabetes are feeling extremely hungry, thirsty and/or tired. Your vision could be blurred or you may need to pass urine more frequently but as these are often general symptoms of pregnancy anyway it is well worth attending your appointments regularly. If gestational diabetes is suspected, you will be given a glucose tolerance test during the second or third trimester. If diagnosed, it can be treated easily and there is no risk to you or your babies.

Vaginal Bleeding

Also known as 'spotting', vaginal bleeding can be worrying but it is surprising how many women pregnant with multiples have experienced it. In their 2008 survey Tamba found that as many as one in four women expecting more than one baby had experienced bleeding at some point during their pregnancy. It often happens during the first trimester, and for some, it can occur irregularly throughout the pregnancy without having any undue effect on the babies. However, it is always best to talk to your health professional if you are experiencing vaginal bleeding so that they can make sure it isn't related to anything else.

Obstetric Cholestasis

Severe itching, usually of the hands and feet, is the main symptom of obstetric cholestasis. This is a pregnancy-related liver condition where the normal flow of bile is diminished. It is thought to be linked to an increase in hormones and therefore is more likely to happen in a multiple pregnancy, usually during the third trimester.

If you are diagnosed with obstetric cholestasis you will be given medication to treat the condition and it is possible that your babies may have to be delivered early. To help with the itching, avoid getting too hot. Wear cool clothes, turn the central heating down and take cool showers or baths. It's best to avoid eating fried or fatty foods and drinking alcohol. Make sure to drink plenty of water. Before going to bed, try soaking your hands and feet in very cold water and apply soothing lotions with calamine, camomile or calendula. OC Support UK (www.ocsupport.org.uk) is a useful website to consult for further information on this condition.

Twin to Twin Transfusion Syndrome (TTTS)

This is a rare condition affecting twins who share a placenta and also some of the same circulation so that blood transfers from one baby to the other. If the first scan shows your twins are sharing a placenta, you will be monitored more carefully for signs of TTTS. Should this be diagnosed, you may be referred to a specialist if your hospital is not able to give the care you need. Tamba have produced a very informative booklet on TTTS and this can be downloaded from their website: www.tamba.org.uk. Further information can be found on the Twin to Twin Transfusion Syndrome website: www.tttsfoundation.org.

Decisions Before Your Babies are Born

Like any new experience it's hard to know exactly what to expect from a multiple birth until it's happened to you. Plenty of people will be prepared to offer you all kinds of advice but at the end of the day, everyone's experiences vary. However, it is always reassuring to know that other mums have been through what you're experiencing and still more are going through it at the same time as you.

There are a number of ways that you can link up with those who already have multiples or are expecting more than one baby. Tamba's website, provides detailed information on multiples and also has a message board. If you're a Tamba member, you can chat online and get a lot of information and support from those who are in the same situation as you. This is particularly helpful once your babies have arrived and you feel as if you're constantly stuck indoors with them. As long as you have internet access at home, there are always people you can reach out to.

Your Birth Plan

When you are expecting twins or more it's a good idea to be as flexible as possible about your birth plan. Talk over the birth arrangements with your partner and health professionals at a reasonably early stage so that you are clear about what is likely to happen during your labour and at the birth of your babies. Even if your pregnancy has been straightforward, you do need to be aware that the chances of complications arising during labour and birth are higher than if you were having one baby. If you set your sights too firmly on one particular plan, you may be disappointed. The most important thing to focus on is the safe delivery of your babies so you may find you need to be open to your health professional's advice.

There are some things that you can have more of a say in, however. For example, indicate whether you intend to breastfeed your babies, whether you would like skin-to-skin contact as soon as they are born, if you want the birth photographed or filmed and any particular music that you would like to listen to while in labour.

There will be a number of health professionals present during the birth but it could be that they don't all have to be there all the time. If you would prefer this to be the case make a note of your preference on your birth plan.

On the following page you will find a sample birth plan that you can use or adapt to your needs.

Tamba Twinline (0800 138 0509) offers a confidential listening service specifically for those with twins or more. It is staffed by trained volunteers who are parents of multiples. Common issues that callers phone about include sleeping, crying, feeding, behaviour and school related issues. The lines are open every day from 10 a.m. to 1 p.m. and again from 7 p.m. to 10 p.m. If you don't have access to a computer or you'd prefer to chat with someone directly, this is a very popular service.

'I first used Twinline when I found out I was expecting twins at eight weeks pregnant just to speak to someone who knew what I was experiencing. Having a three-year-old as well, I was a little concerned at the thought of another two!'

Sample Birth Plan

Due date: Patient of: Midwife: Scheduled to deliver at:	
Labour	
Monitoring	
Induction	
Anaesthesia	
Caesarian	
Episiotomy	
Delivery	
After Delivery	
Feeding	
Support People	
Other	

Organising Help at Home

In most cases having children is a journey you're setting out on with the help of a partner. It's quite likely one of you will have more of the day-to-day care of the babies and although fathers are playing a much larger role these days, it is still generally the mother who plays the biggest part in a child's early life. Having said that, it is really important for both parents to agree on the different aspects of childcare.

For the first few weeks in particular an extra pair of hands at home will be of huge benefit. If you already have other young children, then you really will need more help. Nowadays most men can take a couple of weeks' paternity leave and many opt to take a few more weeks as holiday or unpaid leave. To maximise this time, it may be a good idea for your partner to start his paternity leave once you are home as that's when you will need his help most. With multiples it's more likely that you'll be in hospital for longer than with a singleton. Of course if you already have a child/children at home, this presents other issues.

If your partner's employer is reasonably flexible then they may not insist that paternity leave is booked fifteen weeks before your babies are due but it is worth bearing in mind that this is one of the stipulations of taking paternity leave. It can make things a bit complicated when you're expecting multiples – it is very likely your babies will be born earlier than their due date. Also, you won't know in advance exactly how long you are going to have to spend in hospital. It's worth noting that parents are entitled to up to thirteen weeks' unpaid parental leave for each child under five years of age so long as they have worked with the same company for at least a year. Your partner might consider taking some unpaid parental leave as well as paternity leave. However, it can also be the case that it's not so easy for him to take paternity leave at all. The law has recently changed to allow fathers to take additional paternity leave. This allows you to share the care of your babies if you are planning to go back to work. The leave must be taken after the babies are twenty weeks old and before they turn one.

‘My husband was self-employed and only got paid if he worked so paternity leave was not an option as with baby twins and a growing four-year-old every penny was very much needed. He was able to take the week off work, then my mum took two weeks off and then my sisters took a week between them.’

If friends or family offer to help, accept their kind offers. You may not think that you will need it at this stage but once you're home with your babies you'll probably feel differently. However, make sure helpers do exactly that: it's great to have friends and family popping round to cuddle the new babies and chat with you but, particularly in the first few weeks, you will find that you tire easily and an extra pair of hands helping with cooking and tidying up will be of enormous value.

‘We were in the process of renovating our kitchen when our babies were born (at thirty-five weeks) so the house was in total chaos. My parents saved the day: we moved in with them for a month and it really was the best thing that could have happened. My mum made sure I ate three meals a day and having both my parents to help with the babies really got me back on my feet. I don't know how I would have coped without them.’

If you have no family close enough to help and you don't want to impose on friends it might be worth looking into hiring someone to come and assist you during the initial settling-in period. Plenty of families with newborn twins have benefited from the help of a maternity nurse, a doula (mother's supporter), a nanny, an au pair or a mother's help.

‘We made the big decision to use up all of our "rainy day" money and hired a maternity nurse to come and help with our newborn twins. This gave me more time with our older daughter who wasn't yet two and was the best decision we could have made.’

If your finances won't stretch to paying for someone else to help, try contacting your local branch of Home-Start (www.home-start.org.uk). Home-Start is a voluntary organisation helping families with children under five. What generally happens is that a volunteer will come to your home and help with your babies alongside you. They are usually available for up to four hours once a week. As this is a voluntary organisation it can take a bit of time to sort out a volunteer to help you. It is worth contacting the organisation well in advance of your babies being born to give them enough time to find someone who will be available.

Choosing Names

You may know the sex of your babies before they're born, in which case you may already be using particular names when talking about them. You could be doing this even if you don't know what sex they are. When thinking of names for two or more children, parents sometimes feel they should choose names that have a ring to them – that sound good together, but perhaps not too similar. On the other hand, you may feel that you want names that are totally different to highlight their individuality. Bear in mind how they'll sound in the playground and what their initials might spell! It's funny how often parents can fix on names that somehow just don't seem right when their babies are born so have a few names ready, but don't be surprised if you change your minds when you actually see your babies.

What to Take to Hospital

Have your hospital bag ready in good time as your babies could easily arrive earlier than you think. When packing, bear in mind that you are likely to stay in hospital for a few nights. Tamba has produced a helpful list of items to take with you to hospital and suggests it might be easier to pack three separate bags so you know where to find things: one bag for your labour, one for your stay in hospital and another for your babies.

Bag For Labour

- Facial spray
- Camera with batteries and charger
- List of people to call
- Loose change for car park, phone and hospital café
- iPod or similar
- Books and magazines
- Energy sweets
- Unsweetened juice, water and food for birth partners
- Nightshirt or similar to wear during labour

Hospital Stay Bag

- Breastfeeding nightdresses
- Light dressing gown and slippers
- Socks
- Two loose tops and two pairs of stretchy trousers
- Two nursing bras/two support bras
- Toiletries including deodorant, shampoo, conditioner, make-up, body lotion, lip salve and make-up remover wipes

- Tissues and anti-bacterial wipes
- Hairbrush and hair dryer
- Mirror
- Selection of towels
- Two packs of disposable briefs
- Twenty-four maternity towels
- Pack of breast pads.
- Notebook and pen to record your experience or make notes about the babies. Your first impressions of motherhood will provide fascinating reading for your children in later life

Bag for your Babies

- Newborn-size nappies
- Nappy sacks
- Bag of cotton-wool balls
- Six babygrows and six sleepsuits
- Six vests
- Two shawls/jackets/blankets
- Four pairs of scratch mitts

Notes

Notes

Chapter 2
Birth

'It all happened
very quickly once my
first baby was born.'

It is very likely your babies will be born early. With twins the average delivery is at thirty-seven weeks and with triplets it's at thirty-four weeks (and often earlier with four or more). In 2008, Tamba produced a survey which indicated that 43 per cent of twins and only 1.5 per cent of triplets are born after thirty-seven weeks so if you have reached this stage you are likely to be having your babies very soon! Of course this isn't always the case and some mothers even go past their full term.

‘It was a straightforward twin pregnancy that went to forty weeks plus three days before an induced labour.’

It is far more common for twins to be born prematurely and interestingly, they seem to mature more quickly than singletons do when born early. Also it follows that if they are born earlier, multiples generally weigh less too. The average weight of a single baby is 3.40kg (7.5lb), the average weight of each twin born at thirty-seven weeks is 2.49kg (5.5lb), while the average weight of each triplet born at thirty-three weeks is 1.80kg (4lb) and the average weight of each quadruplet born at thirty-one weeks is 1.40kg (3lb).

‘My first child was born naturally and I was keen to have a natural birth with the twins, but my hospital insisted that it was their policy to deliver twins by Caesarean. As it happened, I went into labour just before the date of my planned Caesarean and they were born naturally after all!’

The way your babies will be delivered does depend quite a bit on their positions towards the end of the pregnancy. If both are in the vertex position (heads down), you are more likely to be able to deliver them vaginally but this is also dependent on your hospital's policy. Tamba statistics indicate that 45 per cent of twins born vaginally are both in the vertex position. If the first child is head down and the second is in the breech position (bottom or feet first), the percentage goes down to between 35 per cent and 40 per cent (and only 10 per cent of vaginal twin births are with both babies in the breech position). Altogether 60 per cent of twin births are carried out by Caesarean and in general most triplets and quadruplets are delivered by Caesarean.

Baby positions

Both vertex

One vertex, one breech

Both breech

One vertex, one transverse

One breech, one transverse

Caesarean (C-section)

More and more doctors seem to prefer multiple birth deliveries to be made by Caesarean and you may well find your local hospital's policy is that they will only deliver multiples in this way (known as a 'planned Caesarean'). If your babies are feet or bottom first (in the breech position), or lying across in the transverse position, it is much more likely your doctor will insist you have a Caesarean. If you have already had a Caesarean with an older child or if your placenta is covering the cervix (known as placenta previa), a Caesarean will also be recommended. An 'elective Caesarean' is when it's your decision to have your babies delivered by Caesarean.

❛I delivered at thirty-six weeks and five days. I was offered the week before but my eldest son's birthday was on that day and requested a Friday as good for all my family and hubby's work and nursery runs, etc.❜

❛I'd had a Caesarean with my first child so chose to have one with the twins – they were born at thirty-eight weeks.❜

Before making your final decision, about whether to elect for a Caesarean, do talk to your GP or midwife about the benefits and risks to yourself and to your babies and what alternatives you may have.

If during labour it becomes apparent you will need a Caesarean, this is known as an 'emergency Caesarean'. It could be because your babies have moved into a difficult position, they may be in distress or the umbilical cord might have dropped into the birth canal before the first baby. It may also be that your blood pressure is too high, the doctors feel your labour is taking too long or the use of forceps or ventouse (a vacuum device) to assist with the delivery is not working.

Many doctors feel that because any one of the above is more likely to happen with a multiple birth, it is advisable to have an epidural so you are prepared in case you do need a Caesarean. An epidural is an injection that numbs the lower part of your body so you won't feel anything in your stomach, pelvic area and legs for a particular length of time. It is administered by a specialist into the lower part of your spine and can be topped up, if necessary. The advantage is that you have total relief from labour pains while still allowing you to be involved.

It is rare for the first twin to be delivered normally and the second by Caesarean – only 5 per cent of all twin births are delivered in this way.

‘As one of my babies was in the transverse position and the other was in the breech position, I was advised to have an epidural in case I needed an emergency Caesarean. As it turned out, they were both born naturally. I now realise how unusual this was and put it down to the fact that they were born in a teaching hospital.’

If you are having an elective or planned Caesarean, you are more likely to be offered an epidural so you are awake throughout the birth of your babies but do not feel any pain. Some women say they can feel some touch or pressure and a tugging feeling. The other advantage to having an epidural is that your partner can be with you throughout the labour. A screen will be raised so you can't see the incision being made – and your partner can opt to be on your side behind the screen. If you prefer not to have the screen, you can request it is removed and that way, you can watch your babies being born.

‘I had an epidural and my husband was able to stay with me the whole time. I requested my own music to be played as well to help me relax and chill out, but the whole experience was very chilled and relaxed and laidback – people chatting to me and my husband and laughing and joking too, which also helped me to feel very relaxed.’

A neat cut will be made at the bikini line and your babies will be delivered fairly quickly. The first baby will be delivered within ten to fifteen minutes and the second baby about two minutes later. If all is well, you will be able to hold them straightaway. The placenta is then delivered and you will be stitched up, which can take up to thirty minutes.

In some cases, if the need arises during labour or if you should go into labour before your planned Caesarean, an emergency Caesarean may be required. If you have had an epidural, this may need to be topped up. Occasionally it might be necessary for you to have a general anaesthetic. If this is the case, your partner may not be allowed to stay with you but should be able to hold the babies immediately after they are born provided all is well with them. Expect a longer stay in hospital if you have had a Caesarean – this is often the case with multiple births anyway, particularly if your babies are born prematurely.

‘Following my C-section, I stayed in hospital for four nights which was only because the boys were jaundiced and needed special care with this and they were very sleepy and lazy feeders.’

Following a Caesarian, a physiotherapist will give you help with exercises to strengthen your muscles and assist in your recovery and you will be told what you can (and cannot) do for the first few weeks. Generally it is recommended you don't lift anything heavy and you should avoid bending down or stretching up. It is advisable to take it easy as much as you possibly can for at least the first month and it is usually recommended you don't drive for a few weeks. However, it is a good idea to try and do some gentle walking to assist with your circulation and prevent the risk of blood clots. Whether or not you are planning to have a Caesarean, it is a good idea to do some research ahead of time in case you do need to have one.

Vaginal Delivery

If this is your first pregnancy you will naturally be wondering how to recognise when you have gone into labour. The difficulty is that the symptoms are not the same for everyone. Having said that, it is likely when the time comes you will know. There are some early signs that your labour may be imminent. You might have a 'show', which is when the mucus plug sealing your cervix comes away, or you may experience 'Braxton Hicks' contractions (weaker, less painful and less regular than full-blown contractions). One of your babies' heads may have become 'engaged' and this can happen up to three weeks before labour starts. You may notice that your 'nesting instincts' have taken over and are suddenly keen to get a lot of housework done. These are all signs to indicate that you could be going into labour shortly and it would be a good time to get your hospital bag packed so you are ready.

When you are pregnant with multiples it is more likely that your waters will break before the onset of labour than when pregnant with one baby. If the waters do break (and this can be anything from a gentle trickle to a gush!), contact your hospital immediately and they will probably advise you to come in right away.

‘ It was my dad's birthday. I was thirty-six weeks pregnant and felt I could treat myself to a little champagne and then my waters broke. We didn't even get to stay to enjoy the rest of the party!’

Induction

If you have not gone into labour naturally, (sometimes as early as thirty-seven or thirty-eight weeks) your doctor or midwife may recommend that you be induced. This could be because they feel either your health or that of your babies is at risk if the pregnancy is allowed to continue beyond this point. Your GP or midwife should explain the reasons why induction is necessary and how they will proceed. The usual procedure is that you will be given a vaginal pessary or gel of prostaglandin to help soften your cervix and encourage contractions to start. If this doesn't happen within twenty-four hours they may need to break your waters manually, which is not usually painful, just a bit uncomfortable. However, if the contractions still haven't begun within a specified time you will be given an intravenous drip of oxytocin (also known as Syntocinon) to get labour started.

First Stage of Labour

When your contractions begin in earnest and as they become more regular and gain in strength, your cervix starts to thin and dilate. This is known as the first stage of labour. Again, with twins or more it is likely you will be asked to go straight to hospital so that your labour can be monitored. A belt with pads and sensors will be strapped to your tummy so that the babies' heartbeats can be checked and your contractions monitored at the same time. It's not the easiest arrangement but you should still be able to move into more comfortable positions with the help of a midwife. Sometimes these belts cannot pick up the babies' heartbeats properly and if that is the case, your first baby will be monitored internally with a fetal scalp electrode attached to the head by a metal clip.

You should have had a chance to discuss pain relief during antenatal classes and your GP or midwife may have advised you to have an epidural because you are having twins or more, as there is always a greater chance you may need a Caesarean. If you have an epidural it is possible to top it up, so you may not have to have a general anaesthetic if the need arises. Your babies' positions also determine whether or not an epidural is recommended. Other forms of pain relief are gas and air or pethidine.

Entonox, gas and air is a colourless, odourless gas made of half oxygen and half nitrous oxide (otherwise known as 'laughing gas'). The idea is that you breathe it in through a mouthpiece or mask as and when you want it and it helps to calm you and takes the edge off the pain of a contraction. It is not harmful to your babies in any way.

Pethidine is a painkilling drug given by injection to help with pain relief and it also helps you to relax at the same time. It can be administered by your midwife. Pethidine should not be given once you are past the first stage of labour as it can affect your babies' breathing (particularly that of the second born) and may make them drowsy for several days afterwards.

Second Stage of Labour

Once your cervix is fully dilated to 10cm (4in) you are at the second stage of labour and are ready to push your first baby out. Some hospitals may have a policy whereby you must be moved into the operating theatre at this stage, however, they should have discussed this with you in advance. They may also prefer you to give birth lying on your back. Again, it is worth discussing this in advance with your GP or midwife so that you are aware of the options. If they feel happy with the way your labour is going, then you may be able to deliver the babies in a position that you find you are better suited to, such as standing, squatting or kneeling on all fours. Should your labour become prolonged and the indication is that your babies are becoming distressed then the doctor may assist with their delivery using either forceps or ventouse. If this is the case then you may need an episiotomy, which is when a small cut is made to the vaginal wall.

Once your first baby has been born, you will be examined to

determine the position of the second baby. It may be necessary for the doctor to change this baby's position, either externally or internally, if for example it is lying in a transverse or breech position.

‘It all happened very quickly once my first baby was born. I only realised afterwards that the second one (who had been in the transverse position) was turned and came out feet first. They were born ten minutes apart.’

It is possible for the second baby to be helped out feet first if it is in the breech position. Normally the second twin is born within twenty minutes of the first and hospital staff will be keen to ensure this is the case. To speed up delivery, you may be advised to have an intravenous hormone drip. Delivering the second child is usually easier than the first because your tissues have already been stretched. Your partner can be cuddling the first baby while you're delivering the second and then it will be your turn to have a cuddle.

Third Stage of Labour

The third (and final) stage of labour is when you deliver the placenta/s. Your GP or midwife will probably recommend you have an injection of Syntometrine, which contracts the uterus and assists in a quicker delivery of the placenta/s. This ensures that there is less risk of high blood loss. If you have had an episiotomy or if your vaginal wall tore, you will now be stitched up. They will almost certainly need to put your legs in stirrups to do this and if you haven't had an epidural, you will be given a local anesthetic first so you don't feel anything while this is happening.

It may be possible at this stage to tell whether your twins are identical or not but it could be that a separate test needs to be carried out and if there isn't a medical need to do so at the time, this might be something you will be recommended to do later on. The easiest way to determine whether your twins are identical is to have their DNA tested by cheek swabs, however, there is generally a charge for this.

Who Will Be Present at the Birth?

There will certainly be more people with you in the delivery room when giving birth to multiple babies than there would be if you were having one baby, and the number will vary depending on your hospital's policy. Again, this is something you might like to discuss with your GP or midwife ahead of time so that at least you are prepared. Generally there will be an obstetrician, an anaesthetist, two midwives and one paediatrician for each baby. In addition, there may be student doctors and junior staff present. If you are not happy to have so many people present at the birth, do talk to your GP or midwife about this and they can request for all non-essential staff to wait outside until required.

However, it is helpful for junior staff to be present so that they can gain good experience. In any case, bear in mind it is quite likely, needing more regular scans and appointments at the hospital, that you will have got to know a number of the staff so they won't all be complete strangers. If everything has gone well, you can always ask that you and your partner and babies are left alone for a bit to take in what you have all been through. However, if you have had a Caesarean then a certain number of medical staff must be present.

Special Care

Because twins and higher multiples are more likely to be born early, there is also a greater likelihood that they will require some form of special care in the first few days or weeks after the birth. In 2008 Tamba carried out a survey of 1,298 mothers of twins and 68 mothers of triplets whose babies had been born within the previous five years. It transpired that 41 per cent of the mothers with twins and 91 per cent of those with triplets said at least one of their babies had to be admitted to the Neonatal Intensive Care Unit (NICU), also known as the Special Care Baby Unit (SCBU).

In order to be prepared for this visit your hospital's NICU while pregnant. Some hospitals are less amenable than others about such visits but it is worth persevering by pointing out that you have a higher chance of one of your babies needing to go there and you may not be in a position to visit them straightaway.

‘One of my babies was admitted to NICU as she had breathing difficulties. Unfortunately I wasn't able to see her for a couple for days as I was on a drip to reduce my blood pressure, which had gone right up after they had been born. I had been advised to visit NICU whilst on a hospital tour and was very pleased I had. I felt much more reassured knowing where she was and that she was in expert hands.’

The NICU is staffed by paediatricians and specially trained nurses and midwives and is equipped with everything necessary for the care of premature babies. If your babies are very small, they may require help to keep their body temperature steady and if this is the case, they will be placed in an incubator. It could be that they have problems with breathing because they are premature and if so, they may be put on a ventilator. Some premature babies are unable to feed in the early days and are assisted either by a tube (which goes through one nostril) or an intravenous drip. There are many other reasons why a baby may need to be looked after in NICU. They may not have to spend too long there, but it is still important for you to visit them as soon as you are able to do so. If you can't get there, ask the hospital staff who else is allowed to go on your behalf – your partner should be able to visit your baby/ies and it may be that other family members such as grandparents will be allowed to go in and they can keep you informed of progress. This could be a stressful time for you and your partner and it is quite normal that you should feel sad, angry or guilty.

What is important is that you feel involved at this stage and there are several ways that you can help. If your baby (or babies) are being fed through a tube, you can express milk for them; it may even be possible for you to breastfeed them. When you visit them, you will be encouraged to use 'kangaroo care' (where you have skin-to-skin contact with your babies by snuggling them into your top against your skin). This is known to speed up recovery as it has a calming effect on them; it also helps with their breathing and heart rate and is a way that you can bond as a family. If you are not able to hold your babies initially, you may still be able to touch them through a porthole in the incubator. They will recognise your voice so you should talk to them softly; they will get to know your smell so you can keep a piece of soft material close to your chest and then leave it with them for reassurance. Ask the hospital staff to tell you how you and your partner can be involved and encourage them to explain the different procedures. You can request that they give you information on progress. It is nice to have photos taken of your babies so you have them with you whenever you are away from NICU.

It could be that only one of your babies goes into NICU and the other one will be with you on the ward. You can always ask if you and the baby can be moved to a ward closer to NICU so that it is easier for you to spend time with each baby. Your hospital may allow you to take the healthier baby with you when you visit NICU and you will find it reassuring to have both babies with you.

'My son had to be in the neonatal unit for ten days but my daughter and I were able to go home after five days. It was very strange as I had the girl with me and we could visit at any time and help feed him.'

Unfortunately there will be occasions when there is simply not enough space in the NICU in your hospital and one or both of your babies have to be transferred to a different hospital for special care. Tamba has been campaigning to draw attention to this problem and is trying to find ways of resolving it because it can be very stressful for the parents involved. In some cases, triplets have had to be cared for in three different hospitals – a logistical nightmare for their parents. The premature baby charity Bliss (www.bliss.org.uk) offers help and support to families with premature babies, as does Tamba. Tamba have recently produced a very helpful booklet, 'Multiple Births – A Parents' Guide to Neonatal Care', which can be downloaded at from their website.

It is common for newborn babies to lose some of their birth weight at first and with multiple birth babies who are often smaller when they are born, hospitals are generally very keen to ensure they have started to gain weight before discharging them from hospital. This may mean that you will be in hospital for a few days and hopefully you can make good use of all the professional help around you. If a private room is available, quite often the hospital will allocate this to you and your babies and it can make a real difference. It is worth asking if a private or smaller room is free once your babies have been born.

'Following their birth, my daughters and I were moved to a room within the maternity wing which we shared with one other mum who had had a Caesarean. I think we were very lucky to have this as it did give us a bit more peace and quiet and I had a bit more space.'

❝I stayed in hospital for four nights after they were born. We were very well looked after and were given our own room for the duration.❞

Who Came First?

Once your babies are born you will probably find that everyone is constantly asking you who came first. This is a natural question but it does carry a lot with it. Having read a number of books during pregnancy, we made the decision not to tell anyone (not even the grandparents!) which child was born first. This was because we didn't want them to be treated differently because there happened to be a few minutes' difference between them. Nor did we want them to have the feeling of being the younger or the older one; right from the start we wanted them to understand they are the same age. We eventually told our twins the full story when they were about ten, as by then, we felt they understood the concept of being the same age and there hadn't been any outside influences to distort this view.

Notes

Chapter 3

Coming Home

'There are two things in
life that you can never be
prepared for: twins.'

Tamba magazine,

October 2009

Even if you haven't been in hospital for too long, coming home with two or more babies can make everything feel so different, particularly if they are your first children. In hospital, you will have had quite a lot of help from midwives and nurses, not to mention all the visitors. Suddenly you and your partner are on your own with two or more little ones who are now about to ensure that you don't get too much time to sit back and relax, let alone have time for shopping or making plans.

Preparation at Home

Equipment

Once you are home with your babies, you are really not going to have any time and so it is worth thinking ahead while you have the opportunity. It's a good idea to identify exactly what you are going to need even if you don't want to buy any major equipment before your babies are born. Tamba produces a very useful buggy guide and has regular product reviews on its website. You can also glean information on an enormous number of baby products from the Internet. It's worth looking around the larger shops stocking baby equipment to see what you might want to buy, but nowadays there is so much on offer and a good deal of it is really not needed. Don't be tempted to buy too much in advance – only go for what is really necessary. It might be possible to buy certain second-hand items through your nearest Twins' Club, or an Internet auction site or, you may even be able to get some for free via websites such as Freecycle in your area. When babies are small, they outgrow certain things so quickly that you will find you can buy items in very good condition and considerably cheaper via these sources.

First Items

- One or two cots or Moses baskets (depending on whether they will be sharing or not)
- Two baby bouncers
- Changing mat
- Nappies: on average each newborn gets through around ten to twelve nappies every day so you will need to bear this in mind when you make your first purchase! As multiples are usually smaller than average at birth, it makes sense to buy the smallest size. At first, you may want to try out different brands on your babies before buying too many of one make
- Baby bath (although while your babies are small, you may find it easier to bathe them in the basin or kitchen sink)
- Buggy
- Car seats
- Baby monitor (depending on the size and layout of your home)
- Blankets and sheets
- Towels
- Muslin cloths
- V-shaped pillow or similar for breastfeeding

' Very little was bought new. I have always bought second-hand privately, in sales or the good old charity shop. I was given a lot of baby clothes and borrowed some small items.'

Friends can often be a great source of baby equipment and you will probably find that because you have more than one baby you will get lots of generous offers. If you are lent cots or Moses baskets it is recommended you buy new mattresses for them. Only accept second-hand car seats from people you know really well. You should be absolutely certain that they haven't been in a car involved in an accident.

It's a good idea to have a few items of clothing ready and you may find that friends are happy to lend you some. Quite often the smallest-size baby clothes hardly ever get worn and if your friends have any of these, they may be very happy to lend them to you. You are also bound to get quite a lot of baby clothes as presents so you might prefer to wait before buying too many in the early months. If there is anyone who doesn't know what to buy, suggest gift vouchers so that you can buy more clothes later when your babies have grown.

'We had a few friends who had already started having families when our two came along and we were amazed at how generous they were, lending us equipment and clothing. It made such a difference.'

Items of clothing you may want to get to begin with are: vests, babygrows, jackets or cardigans, hats, sleeping bags and if it's winter time, snowsuits.

Sleeping Patterns

Your babies can sleep together in the same cot or you may prefer to have them in their own cots. For the first six months it is advisable to have them in the same room as you and for this reason alone, you may find that space dictates you can fit only one cot in. Don't worry: after all, they have been together in the womb and are used to being together and may well find comfort in having each other close by.

'They slept together in the same cot, top and tail. We had no choice as there was no room for two cots as we were living at my parents' house for three months.'

'Whilst we were still in hospital the nurses put our twins into the same cot so we continued doing this once we were home. We had been lent two small cots so when they became too big to fit in together, we separated them.'

‹ *I had to sleep them in the same cot initially as they would not settle without each other. They lay side by side very close to each other, usually their heads touching; they moved there by themselves! They stayed together until they were eight weeks then went into separate cots.* ›

Of course, you may prefer to have your babies in separate cots from day one and if space is an issue, then you might need to be a bit resourceful.

‹ We had a one-bedroomed flat so to start with we put our daughters' cots into a large walk-in cupboard. When they needed more space, they moved into the bedroom and we slept in the sitting room. ›

Current advice is that babies should be placed on their backs with their feet at the end of the cot so they can't wriggle down under the covers. If you are putting two babies into a cot, this can be done with them lying with their feet touching opposite ends of the cot and their heads coming in towards the centre (make sure the cot is long enough to fit them in this way). Otherwise they can be placed side by side with their feet at the same end of the cot. With triplets, you can lay them side by side across the cot. If you want to divide the cot, there are special fixed cot dividers available – don't be tempted to make your own from rolled-up blankets or pillows as these are not safe for small babies. Remember, two or more babies together in the same cot creates extra warmth so check they don't get too hot. Make sure the room is the right temperature, too. The recommended room temperature for sleeping in is between 16 and 20°C (60.8 and 68°F).

Because your babies will be keeping you up during the night while they are still small and need to be fed on a regular basis, it is important that you try and grab some sleep when they are sleeping. The temptation is to use the time to get on with other jobs that you can't manage when they are awake but at this point your main priority should be to get as much rest as you can. Your body has been through some enormous changes and needs time to recover – and then on top of that you're not given much chance to sleep for any 'normal' length of time. Even if you don't sleep when your babies are sleeping during the day, it's still a good idea to relax. Try putting your feet up and dozing; at least this way you're giving your body some rest.

Feeding Your Babies

It's a good idea to take some time before your babies are born to work out whether you want to breastfeed or bottlefeed. Try to obtain as much information as you can in advance and it is definitely helpful to discuss all the options with your partner.

A Tamba survey showed that on average mothers of twins breastfeed their babies for at least twelve weeks. If you can visit your local Twins' Club or at least meet up with another mum with multiples, she will probably be all too happy to answer any questions you may have. For more information, visit the Tamba website or phone Twinline: 0800 138 0509 and see also www.twinsclub.co.uk. The Multiple Births Foundation have recently produced a breastfeeding guide which can be downloaded at www.multiple-births.org.uk. If you can watch another mum breastfeeding twins too, you will find this very helpful.

‘Through my NCT teacher I was put in touch with a mother of twins who had successfully breastfed her babies for ten months. From her I received invaluable advice on many practical issues, before and after the births.’

It is certainly possible to breastfeed twins at the same time but this does require more space and cushions or pillows to help support your babies. As your babies are likely to need feeding eight to ten times every twenty-four hours at first. Try to have some sort of help or support for the early weeks prepare yourself as much as possible in advance.

Reasons to Breastfeed

- Breast milk is definitely the best for your babies as it contains antibodies that they need, particularly in the first three or four months. The initial colostrum (the first 'milk' your breasts will produce) is important for developing the babies' immunity. This creamy substance is rich in fats, protein and antibodies and is easy for the newborns to digest. Your body will produce colostrum for the first few days after which it is replaced by breast milk.
- Breast milk is especially beneficial for premature babies, as it gives them the nutrients they would have got in the womb and helps with brain growth. It is also gentler on their digestive system. As many twins, triplets and more are born prematurely, this is a particularly important consideration.
- You don't have to worry about sterilising bottles and preparing them in advance – your milk is there and at the right temperature (particularly good when travelling). The only extra 'equipment' you need is a properly fitted nursing bra, breast pads and plenty of supportive pillows or cushions.
- Breastfeeding gives you the chance to sit down, relax and cuddle your babies. It is also less likely that you will overfeed them.
- It has been claimed breastfeeding protects against cot death.
- Breastfeeding produces hormones that help your womb contract back to its normal size and also speeds up the post-natal discharge.
- Remember, it's not so easy to hold and bottlefeed two babies at the same time.

Reasons for Bottlefeeding

- If there is someone else who can help you, they could bottlefeed one baby while you feed the other. This is particularly good for your partner as he will feel more involved.
- You will always know exactly how much milk your babies have taken at each feed.
- Bottlefed babies allow you a little more freedom and flexibility as someone else can look after them if you need to go out.
- If you have other small children, it is very often the case that they need you just when you've sat down to feed your babies! This is where your partner can step in and take over the feeding.

‘After trying to breastfeed both my daughters, I found it just wasn't working out as one really wasn't interested. So I breastfed one and bottlefed the other and this worked out fine for us.’

Breastfeeding

The amazing thing is that your body can provide enough milk for two (and even three!) babies but it will need a bit of help. For a start you need to make sure you eat well and drink plenty of fluids. During this time it's a good idea to eat three well-balanced meals each day with healthy snacks in between (fresh fruit and vegetables, wholemeal bread, cheese and yoghurt are ideal). You will find that you get very thirsty when breastfeeding, so make sure you always have a drink handy before you sit down to feed your babies. Water or plain fruit juice are best. You don't have to drink lots of milk to boost your supply but if you find it's hard to keep eating a well-balanced diet all the time, milk will help.

Good-quality ice cream is an excellent source of calcium and you will be burning up a lot of calories through breastfeeding. If you're exclusively breastfeeding twins, it is estimated that you are probably burning up to 1,000 calories each day. Now you have the perfect excuse to eat a whole tub!

It also helps if you can rest at some point during the day. Ideally, particularly when you are first getting your breast milk established, you should try and rest while your babies are sleeping. If you can take a nap even better but if you find that difficult, even sitting down with your feet up will help rest your body. Producing enough milk for two or more babies can be quite a tiring business. Having said that, for some mothers just the act of breastfeeding, once established, is a form of relaxation in itself.

'For me, the real key to managing the demands of motherhood and work existed in breastfeeding itself: breastfeeding forced me to relax, to breathe deeply, to enjoy the babies, and generally to recharge my batteries.'

When you're in hospital it is probably easier to breastfeed one baby at a time as you don't have much space in a narrow hospital bed. However, if you are planning on feeding both babies simultaneously it is advisable to start as early as you can because having two babies sucking at the same time will help your body to understand that this is what is expected of it. Your babies will create double the amount of stimulation and so your body produces double the amount of milk.

There was a very supportive nurse in the hospital who really helped and encouraged me to breastfeed my triplets. I don't think I could have done it without her help.

Sadly not everyone has had the same experience:

'I breastfed for two weeks, then switched to bottle. If I was given more support from the hospital, I would have carried on breastfeeding.'

Some hospitals have special breastfeeding support staff and it is worth finding out in advance if there is anyone who might be able to help you if you are keen to breastfeed. Ask for their details so that you can contact them as soon as your babies are born.

Feeding Your Babies Together

Once you are home you may find that it suits you to feed your babies at the same time. This does not always work out, particularly in the early days but if you are prepared to persevere then you may be able to get them both into the same routine. To begin with, you will probably need someone else to help because if one baby wakes before their feed is due, it is easier if they are not picked up by you. Your babies will instantly recognise your milky smell and this will make them more eager for a feed, whereas if someone else can hold them, they may be distracted for a bit.

‘I was fortunate to have my parents helping me for the first month and if one of my babies woke before they were due to be fed, there was always a doting grandparent on hand to have a little play or a cuddle before the other one woke up.’

You may decide that you would rather feed on demand and this is certainly do-able with twins, but you could find yourself constantly feeding. Some babies can feed very quickly – in which case this may be the way you want to do it. If you feed in this way, you are not so restricted to space either.

‘Having previously breastfed my eldest child for nine months, wanted to do the same for my twins. I started breastfeeding, trying as often as I could to tandem feed, but due to one baby drinking a lot more and the other continually falling asleep during his feed, one twin would always be ready for the next feed about an hour earlier than the other. This mainly happened during the night, which is completely typical. I found myself feeding babies around eight times a night (four each), hence no sleep. I continued to breastfeed for four weeks exclusively after which time my husband had a very direct but sympathetic chat with me, explaining that I was making myself ill and that if I was to feed bottles by night, he could help and I could catch some very much-needed sleep. I spent two days thinking about this and then agreed.*

Expressing Milk

If you are not able to breastfeed both babies at the same time to start with, it is good idea to use a breast pump to encourage the milk supply to get going. The same applies if both babies are not able to feed from you at first. If you can express at the times when you would feed your babies (roughly eight to ten times every twenty-four hours), your body will start to understand the routine. Your hospital may be able to lend you an electric double breast pump or you may feel it is worth getting one of your own. If you want to try one out first, it is possible to hire breast pumps:

Ameda Helpline: 0845 009 1789
(www.ameda.co.uk)
Central Medical Supplies: 01538 399541
(www.breastpumps.co.uk)
The National Childbirth Trust:
(http://nct.org.uk/home) may also be able to help you with breast pump hire.

Using a double breast pump will get your body used to the idea of feeding two babies at the same time. To begin with you may find you don't produce much milk but it is worth persevering as your supply should increase with time.

If you decide that you want to feed your babies at the same time, make sure you have somewhere comfortable to sit, with good support for your back and plenty of space on either side of you so that you can hold both babies. A sofa is ideal, as is your bed. Wherever you choose to go, make sure that you have everything you need to hand so you don't have to get up mid-feed (it's not so easy to do with two!). Cordless or mobile phones and TV remote controls do help to avoid interrupting babies' feeding time.

'Unfortunately, at the time I was breastfeeding we didn't have a TV with a remote control so I would find myself trapped watching programmes that I really didn't want to watch once I'd sat down to feed my twins.'

Breastfeeding Positions

There are many different ways to feed twins at the same time and it's worth trying out the different positions to see which ones you feel most comfortable with.

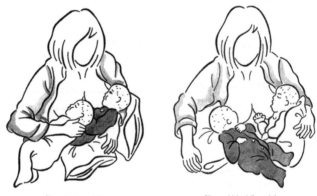

'Parallel' position   'Front V-hold' position

'Football' or underarm position

The 'football' or underarm hold is where you have your babies' legs tucked under your arms and their heads are together. A V-shaped pillow or specially designed cushion is invaluable when feeding this way as it provides additional support for your babies and once you have mastered the technique, you actually have your hands free. To begin with, make sure your pillows or cushions are placed so your babies are on a level with your nipples (their noses should be in line with them). Support their backs and shoulders with your arms and use your hands to bring them to your breasts. At first, it will probably be easier to have someone to help you by holding one baby while you get the other one properly latched on. Once you feel ready, they can pass the other baby to you to latch on. Having done this a few times, you will feel confident to latch them both on at the same time.

‘I always made sure I had my V-shaped pillow with me – it made such a difference. Once I got used to feeding my babies at the same time I even managed to prop a book up at the end of the pillow and that way I could read whilst they fed.’

‘I found sitting on the sofa with an 'Eezenurse' breastfeeding pillow and two bed pillows either side the most comfortable. Holding one baby rugby ball style (baby held under the arm with baby's legs wrapped around your back) and traditional tummy-to-mummy was the best way to feed my boys together.’

Another method is the 'parallel' hold. You will have one baby latched on in the more traditional way, with their legs across your chest and the other is then placed on the other breast, with their legs going in the same direction and tucked under your arm. Again, you need pillows or cushions to help support your babies. At first it is advisable that you latch one baby on at a time but once you feel confident, you will be able to latch them both on simultaneously.

The 'front V-hold' position has your babies facing each other when feeding with their legs in front of you and you use both arms to support their bodies. This is not so easy with tiny babies but it's a good one to use if you're out and about and don't have access to cushions.

Some mothers with twins find it more comfortable to feed their babies lying on their back. This is better to try once you have established the breastfeeding. In this position, your babies can lie so that one is on either side of you.

Whichever way you choose to feed, the most important thing is to make sure you are comfortable, that your back is well supported and you have everything you need to hand. Also, your babies need to latch on properly so they are getting the milk they need without making your nipples sore.

Latching On

It is extremely important that your babies learn to latch on properly and your midwife can help with this. If you are a new mother, it is a good idea to learn how to get them to latch on individually before trying to breastfeed simultaneously. NHS current guidelines are as follows:

Tips for latching on

- Hold your baby close to you with his/her nose level with your nipple. Wait until your baby opens his/her mouth really wide with the tongue down (encourage them to do this by gently stroking their top lip).
- Now bring the baby onto your breast – they will tilt their head back and come to your breast, chin first and take a large mouthful of breast. Your nipple should point towards the roof of their mouth.
- For further information, visit the NHS website (www.nhs.uk) and click on the section called Breastfeeding.

If you are feeding your babies together in bed you will probably find that you and your new family take up all the available space with the extra pillows and cushions that are needed and there is little or no room for your partner. A couple of ways to resolve this problem are either to buy a bigger bed or to position a single bed next to your double so that there is room for everyone. You definitely want your partner to be involved as much as possible and if he is next to you, he can help out by burping the babies, cuddling them and changing their nappies.

Your babies may have very different feeding and sleeping needs and so, even if you would like to feed them simultaneously, this may not always work out. It is a good idea not to have too fixed a plan in mind and to try and work around what is best for all of you. It's possible that you will feed them together for some feeds and separately for others.

Breastfeeding Help

There are a number of organisations who can help further with breastfeeding advice:

National Breastfeeding Helpline: 0300 100 0212

Breastfeeding Network Supporter Line: 0300 100 0210
(9.30 a.m. to 9.30 p.m. every day)
www.breastfeedingnetwork.org.uk

La Leche League Helpline: 0845 120 2918
(www.laleche.org.uk)

Local breastfeeding clinics via your
health centre or midwife/health visitor

NCT Breastfeeding Line: 0300 330 0771
www.nct.org.uk

Association of Breastfeeding Mothers: 0844 4122949
(www.abm.me.uk)

Bliss Special: 0500 618 140
(www.bliss.org.uk)

Tamba Twinline: 0800 138 0509
(10 a.m. to 1 p.m. and 7 p.m. to 10 p.m. every day)

NHS
(www.nhs.uk)

Try and make contact with at least one of the above before your babies are born so that you know exactly who you can get in touch with, should you need help in the initial stages of breastfeeding.

Supplementing with a Bottle

Your milk supply should be properly established by the time your babies are six weeks old. At this point, if you feel that you are not keeping up with their demands or are finding they are becoming fractious at a particular time of day, you could replace one feed with a bottle. It may be that you need to do this if you are going back to work or family demands are such that you just can't breastfeed for every feed. It is worth bearing in mind that it is best to limit the amount of formula your babies are given if you want to continue breastfeeding because they could develop a preference for the bottle and may not feed so happily from the breast. This works the other way round, too. If your babies are used to being solely breastfed, they may not be prepared to take a bottle. It is recommended you introduce a bottle to them at around six weeks so they get used to it. If you decide to do this, you should stick to the same time of day to give your babies their bottles. In this way, your body will easily adjust to the new routine.

❝I used to find by the evening I didn't feel as if I had much milk to offer my babies. It was also the time that my husband was home so he could help with a bottle feed.❞

Should You Use the Same Breast?

There are differing opinions on whether you should keep one breast for each baby or alternate at each feed. There are definitely situations where one baby demands more than the other and to some extent the milk supply in each breast is independent so it might make sense to reserve one breast for each child. You may feel a bit lop-sided if you do this, but it's unlikely that anyone else will notice! Particularly to begin with, one of your babies may not suck so strongly as the other and if this is the case, it is probably better to swap them round so that both breasts are similarly stimulated and your milk supply encouraged equally. There is also the argument that if you always feed your babies on the same side, they only get one perspective and it might be better for them to be alternated.

Breastfeeding Premature Babies

Even if your babies are premature and are in the neonatal unit being fed through a tube, you can still produce milk for them by expressing. In fact, they will benefit hugely from breast milk. If you want to do so, let the staff know so that they can help you to achieve this. It is a good idea to try and use the 'kangaroo care' method (where you have as much skin-to-skin contact with your babies as possible) as this will also help to stimulate your milk supply.

Breastfeeding Triplets

If you are expecting triplets it is even more likely that they will spend some time in the neonatal unit and therefore it makes sense to talk to the staff at the hospital before your babies are born to let them know you are keen to breastfeed. It is certainly possible to breastfeed triplets and there are many mothers who have done so. Your body's supply-and-demand capability for breast milk production can ensure that you have enough milk to feed your babies but you will have to work quite hard to achieve this and be prepared to put in the time it takes. For a start, you must make sure that you eat plenty of healthy foods drink far more water or fruit juice than you usually would and get adequate rest.

If you are able to talk to someone who has breastfed triplets or more (or better still, if they are able to show you how they do it), you will find this extremely helpful. Tamba has a Supertwins group for families with triplets or more and they may be able to put you in touch with someone who can help you.

You certainly will need to have help, especially at the beginning. If your partner is able to take a good stretch of time as paternity leave, this would be ideal. Otherwise contact anyone who you feel is experienced, reliable and able to give some of their time. Alternatively you may find it best to employ someone to help out.

It is worth contacting a breastfeeding counsellor to get their initial advice and have their phone number handy so that you can call on them if you need some help or support.

Positions for Breastfeeding Triplets

There are so many different options for breastfeeding triplets and with time you will work out which option (or options) suit you best.

- You can breastfeed two babies together and bottlefeed (with expressed milk) the other propped up next to you.
- Or you might prefer to express your milk and share it out between them.
- Taking turns, you can breastfeed two babies together and then breastfeed the third on both breasts.
- You might opt for feeding each one separately and if they don't take too long over their feeds, this can work out well.
- Another method is to breastfeed one and bottlefeed the other two with expressed milk.

It is probably a good idea to have some kind of system to record which baby has been fed in which way so that you can be sure to feed them all fairly.

Just knowing that it is possible to breastfeed multiples can be the boost you need to achieve it, but having the right sort of support and encouragement makes a huge difference. There are no fixed rules: do what feels right and what you feel works best for you and your babies. Take one day at a time and remind yourself that you're doing an amazing job.

❛I breastfed all three successfully: one for six months and two for a year. During pregnancy I contacted Tamba and spoke to another mother who had breastfed triplets. She sent me various articles written by other mothers who had breastfed, so I knew it was possible and I was determined to give it my best shot despite being deterred by health professionals whilst in hospital.❜

Bottlefeeding

At first, when your babies are still small and unable to support themselves it may be hard to get the hang of bottlefeeding and it will take a bit of time for you to find out what works best for you and your new family. If you have someone else at home who can help, bottlefeeding is not a problem as you can each feed one baby. It might be a good idea to alternate which baby you feed so you have one-to-one time with each of them.

If you are on your own, you may find it easier to bottle feed one at a time to begin with while you get the hang of it and it may be your babies are in a routine that allows for this. If you want to feed them both together (or better said, if they are *demanding* to be fed at the same time!), there are several different positions that you can try out.

Some Bottlefeeding Positions

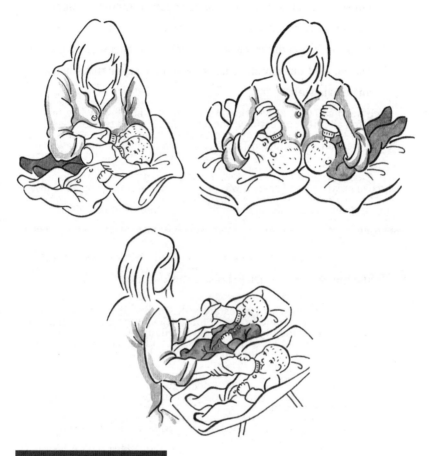

Bottlefeeding Positions

- You can sit on the sofa with one baby on each side of you, either with their bodies parallel to your legs, with their heads facing you and slightly raised by cushions, or with their heads resting on each of your thighs so that you can hold the bottles for them. You can use the same positions when you're in bed propped up by pillows.

- Try propping them up in bouncy chairs or car seats and have them in front of you so that you can hold the bottles for them. This position does mean you don't have any physical contact but you can still talk to them. Otherwise you could alternate by holding one child and having the other in a car seat in front of you.

- When you're out and about, you can sit between your babies in the car and feed them propped up in their car seats or feed them while they are in their buggy.
- If you need to use something to help prop a bottle up while feeding your babies that's fine as long as you are always with them. There are various hands-free feeding systems that you might find helpful (see www.podee.com), but your babies need to be used to being bottle fed before you try any of these.

As they get older and stronger, bottle feeding becomes easier and they will soon learn to hold the bottle for themselves from quite an early age.

More equipment is needed for bottlefeeding and it is suggested you have at least twelve bottles as some will be in the steriliser while you're using others. It makes sense to buy the larger bottles and save money because you will need them later on. To begin with, you won't be filling them up but it won't be long before your babies manage to finish a full bottle! Teats come in different shapes and sizes depending on the size of your babies and what their preferences are. This might require a bit of trial and error to start with. You will need a special brush to clean the bottles with, a steriliser and either expressed or formula milk to suit your babies' needs.

Postnatal Depression

In 2008 Tamba carried out a Health and Lifestyle Survey and found that mothers with multiples have a higher risk of getting postnatal depression (PND) than those with singletons. In fact, one in five mothers with multiples had been diagnosed with PND and a further one in five thought they may have experienced it. The condition can be treated with prescribed medication or through counselling or therapy but the important thing is to recognise the problem and seek help. This is not a condition that you can just 'pull yourself together' to resolve. Unfortunately some people still feel there is a stigma attached to PND and we need to increase awareness that it is an illness and one that requires proper treatment.

PND should not be confused with the 'baby blues', which many new mothers do experience soon after the birth of their babies. One of the main differences is that this only lasts for a few days whereas PND doesn't just go away. In rare cases, PND can start during pregnancy, but more commonly occurs after your babies have been born with some mothers report the problem starting several months after the birth. There are rare cases of fathers getting PND, too.

There are a number of symptoms including feeling miserable, finding it hard to concentrate, being very tearful, having no energy, not being interested in yourself, your babies or your partner, getting anxious or easily irritated, feeling like you're a bad mother, that you're a failure, not wanting to see friends, not sleeping or eating well. You may experience some of these symptoms and not be suffering from PND but if they persist and you're at all concerned, or if family or friends notice you are not yourself, it is advisable to seek medical advice. Your midwife, health visitor or GP are the best people to contact. If you do need treatment for PND, your babies will be taken into account.

It is important to understand that PND *can* be treated; there is medical help. Remember, it's not a sign that you are not a good parent and the chances are your babies will be unaware of what you've been through. With the right help and treatment, you *will* get through it. In some cases, mothers who have suffered from PND have commented that it changed them for the better: they were able to recognise its symptoms in other mums and were able to help by calling on their own experiences. As the Tamba PND guide states: 'PND is not the end – there is life afterwards'.

Sometimes just being diagnosed with PND comes as a relief. At least there is a medical reason to explain why you have been feeling so wretched. Accept any offers of help, both practical and emotional, from family and friends who you know will be supportive. Home-Start may be able to help; if not, you might feel you need to hire some help for a while.

How Can I Help Myself?

The sudden arrival of two or more babies in your life can present you with many new practical, emotional and financial challenges that may be overwhelming. Follow the suggestions below to keep yourself focused and on top of your new life:

- Talk to others
- Take exercise
- Be realistic
- Try to rest
- Do things you enjoy
- List things to do
- Mix with other mums

Some Other Ideas for Support

- **Tamba** have produced 'Postnatal Depression: A Guide for Mothers of Multiples', a booklet which is available online

- Tamba's helpline, **Twinline**, is on 0800 138 0509 and the lines are open every day from 10 a.m. to 1 p.m. and 7 p.m. to 10 p.m.

- **The Association for Postnatal Illness (APNI)** are online at www.apni.org or call 020 7386 0868

Meet-A-Mum Association (MAMA) at www.mama.co.uk
Family Welfare Association at www.fwa.org.uk
Mental Health Matters at www.mentalhealthmatters.com

Notes

Chapter 4
First Year

'Advice I was given
was to take one day
at a time.'

Individuality

'Although we look alike, there is a me within.'

If your twins are identical, you will need to work at telling them apart.

'I hate to admit it, but there were times when I'd pick one of my daughters up and call her by her sister's name, thinking that was who I had in my arms!'

It could be that your babies are slightly different in weight (which can make quite a difference when they are newborn), their cries may vary or one might have a birthmark to help identify them. Should you have none of these differences, you may decide to dress them in particular colours so that you know who is who. If you decide to do this it's fine while they are very little but as your children get older, you don't want them to become dependent on always wearing particular colours.

'As a way of helping to identify our identical twins, friends and family would focus on their shoes (once they were walking). They tended to share clothes but would always have their own shoes on, so I made a point of buying them in different colours to help.'

There is often the temptation to dress multiples alike and this is really not a problem when they are very young – other than it could present you with more work. If someone has kindly given your babies identical outfits, there is no harm in dressing them up when your friend comes to visit but you will make life easier for yourself if you don't feel tied into dressing them identically. It is important to encourage individuality as early as possible and if you get your children into a pattern of feeling they always have to be dressed the same, it will certainly not be helpful.

As well as you and your partner agreeing to treat your children as individuals, it is important that you should encourage other family members and close friends to do the same. Ask that they don't call them 'twins' but always make a point of calling them by name. The same applies to anyone else involved in their care such as a nanny, childminder, or teacher.

There is a unique and very special relationship between twins but it shouldn't be the most important aspect of their life. Professor Pat Preedy, Tamba's Education Research Consultant divides multiples into the following categories:

- **Closely Coupled**: where they are very much a unit and tend not to make their own friends. They dress and behave the same and will answer to each other's names. They are more likely to have their own language (known as cryptophasia or cryptoglossia).
- **Extreme Individual**: where they really don't like being a multiple. They tend to be very competitive, are extreme opposites and would certainly never dress alike.
- **Mature Dependence**: which is the ideal model, where they are individuals and have their own identity. They have both separate and shared friends and support their twin. Each is comfortable being the same or being different.

‘My two boys are so competitive with each other that I'm finding it really difficult right now. They seem to prefer doing things separately, too.’

It is important that you help your multiple children to achieve mature dependence. Always use their names and try hard not to compare them. Twins are particularly sensitive to this and will gain more confidence if encouraged individually from an early age. Try to factor in one-to-one time. When they are very little this can be during nappy changing or bathtime but make sure you have as much eye contact with them as you can.

As your children get older, it is a good idea to organise separate playtimes with friends and to give them each different experiences so that they are not always doing the same activities. If you have the space let each have their own bedroom; this is ideal, otherwise encourage them to have their own areas of a shared bedroom and if possible allow them to choose what they have there and how it is decorated.

Early Days

Even if you already have other children those first months at home with twins (or more) will certainly be a new experience for you and if they are your first, the experiences will all be even more unfamiliar. There will be ups and downs.

It may be hard, but the more organised you are, the easier things will be for you. Many people with twins have said that the only way they coped in the first months was to have some sort of routine. Having said that, it's probably better not to be too strict with yourself as far as this is concerned because babies' routines do change and often this seems to happen just when you've started to adapt to the latest one.

Try not to expect too much of yourself. You're already feeding and caring for two (or more) additional members of the family, which will certainly be a huge change. Work out your priorities – and keeping the house tidy shouldn't come too high on the list! Not all housekeeping tasks are essential, are they?

‘Advice I was given was to take one day at a time, but I would say to anyone having triplets that in those early months, you should take one *hour* at a time!’

The main things to concentrate on are feeding and caring for your babies as well as giving yourself time to devote to them and any other children already in your family. You also need time to focus on yourself: to make sure that you are eating well, getting sufficient rest and finding time to share with your partner. If you feel well then looking after your babies will be so much easier.

Help at Home

If you're lucky enough to have offers of assistance from friends or family do accept them, but make sure that they do come to help. It's easy to feel that you have to entertain visitors but at this stage it's just not practical. Before helpers arrive, think of jobs that they can do and reward them with time to cuddle your little ones!

Fathers/partners will be your main help and with the demands of twins or more, they will find that they become much more involved than if there was just one baby. Grandparents are another wonderful source of help and are often willing to come and lend a hand, sometimes even at short notice. However, you may be in a situation where you don't have family or friends close by, or they may not have the time or physical capability to give you the help occasional. If this is the case there are alternatives. Unfortunately having twins and even triplets does not automatically qualify you for extra help from Social Services. If you have quads or more, you should definitely contact social services.

Nannies

If you can afford to pay for help, consider hiring a nanny either part-time or full-time. Nannies are professionally trained for their qualification or they may have learnt on the job and so the rate of pay will vary. Some prefer to live in while others are happy to come on a daily basis. It is sometimes possible to do a nanny share with a friend, if you don't require or cannot afford a full-time nanny.

Finding a Nanny

There are a number of websites covering nanny hire. Norland Nannies (www.norlandagency.co.uk; 01225 904030) is probably the most well known. Often *The Lady* magazine advertises placements and it is always worth checking your local papers. When you hire a nanny, you become an employer and are therefore required to pay tax and National Insurance; nannies also have holiday entitlement. If you go through a reputable agency, they will have the most up-to-date information concerning this and will have established whether the nannies they recommend to you have the appropriate visas, if from abroad, and qualifications such as prior experience working with multiples. It is always a good idea to contact any referees prior to hiring. You may also find it helpful to have a paid trial day with a prospective nanny so you get a better idea of how they interact with your children.

Au Pairs

If you have a spare room at home you might consider having an au pair to provide you with an extra pair of hands at certain times of the day. Au pairs usually come from abroad to study English and so will need free time to attend college. Bear in mind that they are not generally experienced in childcare so shouldn't be left on their own with small babies unless you are absolutely confident in their ability. However, they can certainly help you with your children when you're there and they may be given light jobs around the house. Otherwise you might prefer to employ a cleaner or other domestic help so that you have more time to devote to your babies.

> *We didn't have the money when the babies were first born but as soon as we did, we employed a cleaner to come and help in the house and that has made such a difference. I'd definitely say she's been a very good investment.*

Registered Childminders

Childminders work in their own homes and are registered to look after a maximum of six children under the age of eight. However, they are not usually registered to take care of more than one child under the age of twelve months. If you are interested in employing a childminder to look after twins or more under this age, they can apply for a special registration to do so. It is also possible for them to request special registration to allow them to work in your home, if that is what you and they decide is preferable. Childminders charge per child and some may offer a discount for twins – it is always worth asking! Visit the National Childminding Association's website at www.ncma.org.uk for further information.

Day Nursery

Intended for the care of children of working parents, day nurseries will look after your children either full- or part-time. They usually offer a discount if you have more than one child in their care.

Home-Start

Home-Start (www.home-start.org.uk) is a voluntary organisation that helps families with children under the age of five. Most volunteers have families themselves, so have been through the experience of having small children and are able to offer up to four hours' help a week in your home. This may not sound like much, but it is amazing what a difference it makes knowing you are going to have that regular weekly visit: someone to chat to, someone to give you a hand with the children and you know they are there for you. Home-Start has helped many families with twins, triplets and more as they are definitely seen as families who qualify for the help that it can offer. Because Home-Start is a voluntary organisation relying on local volunteers, it can take time to be matched with someone so it's a good idea to contact your local branch before your babies are born if you feel that you would benefit from their help.

'I contacted our local branch of Home-Start when I was pregnant with triplets as I knew we couldn't afford to pay for any help at that time. I was very lucky to get two wonderful older women who took it in turns to come and help me for a few hours once a week. It made such a difference to have another pair of hands to help me to feed them or to enable us all to go shopping, go to a playgroup or similar. Just getting out of the house was hard to manage on my own when they were little.'

'There's only eighteen months between my eldest son and the twins and when they were all little, I really appreciated having a Home-Start volunteer to help me. We would often take them all to the local park, which they loved – and I enjoyed getting out too.'

Nursery Nurse Training Colleges

Often nursery nurse training colleges like their students to get work experience while studying and families with twins, triplets or more can be an ideal source of work experience for them. An organisation called Cache (0845 3472123, www.cache.org.uk) can provide details of colleges in your area that teach the relevant courses. Make sure any student coming to help you is doing a Level 3 Diploma in Childcare and Education – they will then be suitably qualified to help you with your little ones. However, you won't be permitted to leave your children alone with a student, but he/she can certainly provide an excellent additional pair of hands.

‘Over the years I had five different students who came and helped us. Some were wonderfully helpful but with a couple it was more like having another child around!’

Even if you don't think that you will need help with your babies do accept offers from those close to you. Sometimes just having another adult to chat to and muck in while you go about caring for your little ones can make a big difference to your day.

Safety Note

Appointing a carer for your children, requires careful consideration. Talk it over with your partner so that you both have a chance to say what you are looking for and where possible, try and get recommendations from friends or family. You should be very clear about your expectations so that you can discuss these when interviewing. Ideally you need someone who has experience of looking after twins or more. Your local Twins' Club may provide some useful contacts.

At the time of writing, it is not a legal requirement for nannies to have a CRB (Criminal Record Bureau) check, but if they have come through an agency it is most likely that this will have already been carried out. Childminders, however, must be registered and are routinely inspected by Ofsted (www.ofsted.gov.uk).

Keep It Simple

At Home

There are all sorts of ways in which you can save yourself time and if you focus on keeping things as uncomplicated as possible this will help. Choose clothes that are easy to get on and off so you don't spend time on fiddly fastenings (babies will happily stay in their babygrows all day). Of course it's fun to dress them up, but you don't need to do this every day – save it for special occasions. Make sure that your babies' clothes (and your own!) are machine washable and don't require ironing – the last thing you want is to have to handwash or iron clothes as well as everything else you're doing.

- Keep nappy changing items downstairs so you don't have to keep on going upstairs every time you need to change one of the babies.
- During the day you may find it easier to give your babies their naps downstairs. Moses baskets or prams can be used for this purpose.
- It's not essential that your babies have a bath every day. Chances are you are keeping them clean after each feed and nappy change anyway!

Shopping

Try and do your bulk shopping online: going to the supermarket with twins or more is not an easy thing to do on your own. If you do need to go shopping with your babies, you will soon discover which shops are double buggy friendly. These will be the ones that you visit when you have your children with you and the others will have to wait! If you really have to go with your babies visit during quiet times and you will find that the staff will be more amenable to giving you a hand. If you have someone to help you, take them along but even better (if they are suitably qualified), leave them at home to look after the babies. Some of the larger supermarkets can even provide triplet trolleys, but you will have to order one in advance. When you take your babies out shopping, be prepared for it to take a while – other shoppers will stop to admire your family and want to chat. It's one of the hazards of being a parent with multiples!

Getting Out

As much as possible be organised so you know where everything is and that way you won't be spending precious time hunting for keys, when your babies are finally dressed and ready to go out. Have your nappy bag ready – try and keep it stocked up with nappies, changes of clothes, baby wipes – so that it's ready if you need to leave in a hurry. It's handy to keep a few little toys and a bit of money in this bag, too – just in case.

You will need to take your babies to be weighed regularly. Initially, the health visitor may be happy to do this in your home. However, if you have to go to the clinic, find out when it's likely to be less busy or whether it is possible to make an appointment to avoid waiting. It will help if a friend or family member is able to go along with you as another pair of hands – your babies have to be totally undressed, weighed and then dressed again, and there may not be enough staff members at the health centre to help you. This is definitely a time to dress your little ones in babygrows or similar clothing that is easy to get on and off.

'When my twins were little, I was very lucky to get help from both my mother and my mother-in-law. I would try and organise their visits to coincide with the day we needed to go to the health centre so that I had someone to help me if they needed to be weighed or vaccinated. It made such a difference to have an extra pair of hands on these occasions.'

If you are lucky enough to have a Twins' Club not too far from where you live it is worth trying one of their drop-in sessions. For one thing, it can be very reassuring to get together with other parents who are going through the same experiences as you are. Twins' Clubs are also a good source of helpful tips on how to cope with two or more babies. It's amazing how resourceful people become when they need to and interesting to hear how they manage.

'I contacted my local Twins' Club when I was pregnant with the twins. They put me in touch with a couple of other mothers who had already had one child before having twins, which was the situation I was in. It was so reassuring to be able to chat to them.'

Twins' Clubs can also be a useful source of secondhand baby equipment and unless you really want to splash out and buy everything new, it does make sense to get certain items secondhand – partly because you're not going to need them for all that long and for that same reason they probably haven't been used much and will therefore be in relatively good condition. A playpen is a good example of this. It does take up space but you can pop two or more babies in at the same time and there will be occasions when you have to step out of the room for a moment and want to know your children are going to be safe. Playpens can also be useful in the garden or as a place for a daytime nap. It is not advisable to leave children in them for too long, though, as they do need more outside stimulation too.

There is a huge variety of baby equipment on offer and it's very easy to be tempted into buying too much. Chat to other parents of twins before making expensive purchases and find out whether it really is worth spending your money in this way. If you can buy good-quality items secondhand for a reasonable price – or better still, if you can borrow certain items of equipment – it is worth doing so as you will find that your babies will outgrow both clothes and equipment quickly.

Nappy Rash

Unfortunately, nappy rash is one thing your babies are likely to succumb to at some point. It's caused by urine or faeces coming into contact with the skin under their nappy and as a result, their bottoms can become red and sore. Nappy rash generally occurs between nine and twelve months. If you catch it early, it can be quickly treated. Make sure the nappies your babies are wearing are sufficiently absorbent and change them regularly, too (you may want to try a different brand of nappy which is more absorbent).

When changing nappies, avoid using soap as it can cause irritation to sensitive skin; wash your baby with warm water and make sure you dry him/her gently but thoroughly. Whenever possible, try to leave your babies' nappies off for some time so their skin benefits from fresh air. Using a proper barrier cream helps prevent nappy rash. *Talcum powder can aggravate it.*

If nappy rash persists or becomes painful, you should consult your GP. Sometimes nappy rash can be caused by a bacterial infection which will require medical treatment, so don't let it go on for too long.

Sleeping

For the first six to eight weeks babies' sleeping and eating patterns are usually hard to predict. On average newborns will sleep for between sixteen and twenty hours each day and this goes down to about fifteen hours a day once they are around four months old. At approximately six months they may be able to sleep for up to twelve hours a night, but will probably wake occasionally during this period and then take a couple of naps during the day as well. By the time they reach one year they will still be having morning and afternoon naps and sleeping a total of about fourteen hours each day.

The figures above are a rough guideline and it is likely your babies won't always stick to them. You must also take into account whether they were born prematurely as their development may not be at the same stage as a baby born at forty weeks. It is all too easy to compare your children's sleeping habits with those of other people's babies of a similar age but you will soon realise that they all have different sleep patterns and it is best not to expect your babies to be doing the same.

You can help your babies by giving them the opportunity to sleep. There are times when they can be overstimulated and then find it hard to doze off. During the day you may find it easier to have them in a Moses basket or carrycot nearer to you and at night they can be in their cot/s.

Tips for Helping Your Babies Sleep

- Ensure your babies are wearing comfortable clothing when they are going to sleep. It should fit properly and must not be too tight anywhere. Baby sleeping bags are very popular.

- If your babies have been in Special Care for some time, they will most likely already be in a routine and it's a good idea to stick to this if you can. Otherwise you may want to try and establish some sort of routine as early as possible – most parents with two or more babies find this makes a big difference. Do take into account that not all babies need the same amount of sleep: they do all need to sleep but, for example, the average sleep needed by a one-month-old is sixteen hours. however this can range from nine to nineteen hours and there will be times when you find it varies from day to day.

‘The twins slept in different places in the day (pram or carrycot) and it was the cot for night-time.’

In the early months you may find your babies sleep for longer stretches during the day than at night and this is fine: you want them to learn how to sleep. Try and create a different atmosphere for their day and night-time sleep routines. At night, keep everything much calmer by having the curtains drawn and turn the lights down low. Think about what fits in best with the rest of the family, too. If you have older children, you may want to get the younger ones into bed a bit earlier so that you can spend some time with them. You may find one of your babies needs more sleep than the other and therefore it works better to stagger their bedtimes. This will give you the chance to spend one-to-one time with each of them.

Cot Death

Quite naturally, most new parents are concerned about cot death. It is still not known why this happens, however, it is a rare occurrence. The NHS offers the following guidelines to help reduce the risk as much as possible:

- Place your babies on their backs to sleep in a cot. They should be in the feet-to-feet position (with their feet at the end of the cot). The same advice applies to prams.
- Have your babies sleep in the same room as yourself.
- Do not smoke during pregnancy or allow anyone else to smoke in the same room as your babies.
- Do not share a bed with your babies if you have been drinking alcohol, if you take drugs or if you are a smoker.
- Never sleep on a sofa or armchair with your babies.
- Keep your babies' heads uncovered. Their blankets should be tucked in no higher than their shoulders. Do not let them become too hot.

Crying

There are numerous reasons why your baby (or babies) may be crying. When they are small, hunger is usually the main reason but it could also be that they have a dirty nappy, they might be feeling uncomfortable, or too hot, or too cold, they may be too tired or they could even be unwell. If one of your babies starts to cry, it doesn't always follow that the other one will do the same. In fact, some parents have noticed the opposite.

‘It was almost as if they were taking it in turns. If one cried, the other often didn't and vice versa. I sometimes felt they realised if one cried, they'd get some attention.’

Of course, there will be times when both babies are crying simultaneously and this can be hard to cope with if you are on your own and cannot identify the reason why. Sometimes just the sound of your voice can soothe them initially or a gentle touch will reassure them that you are there. There will be times when you need to pick them both up: you can put one on each shoulder or lie them both across your lap. While they are small this isn't difficult but as they grow, so too will your muscles! You might find it helpful to pop one child into a sling while you carry the other if there isn't anyone else around to give you a hand. Some parents have even managed to put two slings on at the same time (at a diagonal angle), but to save your back this probably only works when babies are very small. In time you will learn what helps to soothe them, but you may need to try out a few different positions first.

A change of location can provide the necessary distraction – just moving into a different room, going out in the garden or looking out of the window can help. Alternatively, putting both babies into their pram/buggy and going out for a walk may calm everyone down, including you. Some parents find that at certain times of the day the only solution is to take their babies out for a drive. It's wonderful the way the motion of the car can quickly soothe a crying baby.

Comfort

Some babies will have already learnt to suck their thumb while still in the womb and will use this to comfort themselves. In some ways this is ideal as it's always there for them. Others find comfort in a blanket, a piece of soft fabric or a special cuddly toy.

Having twins or more means that your babies are not always going to be able to have your full attention and there will be times when you need to deal with one while the other waits. Some babies just seem to want to suck something for comfort, not because they want more milk, and many parents of multiples have found that using a dummy can help enormously. Try not to use them too often and maybe just when you're at home. *Never dip them into something sweet to make them tastier as this will affect the development of their teeth.* Dummies must be kept clean and sterilised, particularly when babies are very small. Never tie a dummy round a baby's neck. They often come with a clip that can be safely attached to clothing. Not all babies automatically take to dummies (and some never will) but if you feel that you would all benefit from the promise of peace, it is worth persevering for a bit. As they get older it is a good idea to lessen the amount of time they use a dummy as it can interfere with the development of their teeth and speech.

They used dummies at times during the day, when I was trying to prepare their food or when I was cooking dinner, and particularly when I was driving. I always removed them before bed as I didn't want them to rely upon sucking themselves to sleep. At six months old they spat them out and didn't want them any more. Now they both suck their thumbs when they are tired.

I tried to get them to take dummies as I felt they might help occasionally, but neither of them was interested.

If your babies have adopted a blanket or cloth as a comforter, try and get them to use one that can be cleaned easily and replaced as necessary. The same applies if they have their favourite cuddly toys. The last thing you want is to be away from home and find that you've come without the comforter and nothing else will do.

Weaning

Current feeding guidelines suggest you wait until your babies are six months old before introducing them to solid foods. Milk will still be their main source of nutrition at this stage so weaning can be done slowly and in that way they will get used to the texture and taste of foods first. If you feel that they are ready to be weaned earlier, it is best to check with your health visitor or GP first and if they were premature, it may be advisable to wait a little longer. There are various indicators that your babies are ready for solid foods. If, having stopped waking in the night and wanting to be fed, they start up again then they may be ready to be weaned; they may also show an interest in the food you're eating. It also helps if they can sit up. You may feel that one child is ready to be weaned before the other and that's fine. If so, wean one first – the other one will follow soon enough.

Learning to eat is a messy process and when you're teaching two or more babies, the mess will definitely be greater! Be prepared for this and don't let it become a stressful event for you or your babies – you want it to be fun. It doesn't matter if they don't eat much to begin with as they are still getting what they need from their milk. Get everything you're likely to need to hand before you get started. Have them dressed in clothes you don't mind getting dirty – if it's summer and nice and warm, they could be stripped down to vests and nappies. It's a good idea to use large bibs – the plastic pelican ones are probably best as they catch anything that doesn't get eaten and are easy to empty and clean. To start off with, you might prefer to use muslins tied round their necks as these are softer, easy to wash and large enough to cover most of your baby. When you first start feeding them, pop them in their bouncy chairs, car seats or pushchairs, having first covered the floor with something protective – newspaper is ideal as it can be thrown away afterwards.

❝We kept bouncy chairs in our bedroom and fed our twins their breakfast in them at first as they always seemed to be desperately hungry in the morning. We kept their baby car seats downstairs and they'd have their other meals in those.❞

When they are a bit older and able to sit up easily, you may prefer to transfer your babies to highchairs. The type of highchair you choose will depend on how much space you have at home, but they can be very useful when you want to keep your little ones in a secure place for a short time once they are able to sit up. You must always be with them when they are in their highchairs and you are advised to harness them in as it's amazing how quickly children learn to stand up in highchairs.

There are all sorts of highchairs available and it is a good idea to think carefully about exactly what you need before going ahead and buying them. If you don't have a lot of room, you can get highchairs that fold flat and may be tidied away when not needed. Others can be attached to your table by clipping or there are higher chairs that don't have their own tray: your children will use the table to eat from and in this way they become part of the family group at mealtimes. When you're away from home there are a number of options, from folding clip-on highchairs to material harnesses attached to chairs to keep your children secure. If you're using clip-on chairs, make sure the table is strong and sturdy enough to take them.

When you begin feeding your babies, you only need one bowl and one spoon – they will already be used to sharing and this makes it a lot easier for you. While one is swallowing what you've just given them, you can be giving the other their spoonful. Let them touch and play with their food as that way they will learn about it. You can also give them each a spoon to hold while eating so that they get used to it. They will soon be ready to try finger foods and you want to encourage this, too.

❛I had two multi-position highchairs and would sit opposite them to feed them with one bowl of food and one spoon between them. I always gave them a spoon to hold themselves and some finger food to play with. They went on to solids at six months old.❜

It is a good idea to offer your babies a wide variety of recommended food over time so that they get used to different textures and flavours. If you're unsure of which foods to start with, ask your health visitor for advice: breastfed babies will have already sampled many different tastes from your milk but if they're fed on formula, their tastebuds won't be so used to changes. And if they don't seem to be interested in a certain food the first time you offer it, try again on another day. There will be times when they reject what you think will be delicious for them. Try not to be disheartened when this happens as they may love it the next time it's offered.

It's probably best not to go to too much effort when preparing food for babies in the early days as it can be upsetting when they reject it after lots of hard work on your part. To make things easier on yourself, cook a few meals at a time, blend it all, quickly cool what you don't need that day and freeze it in small containers. For single babies it is suggested that you freeze their food in ice-cube containers, but with multiples you will probably find that you need something larger like a yoghurt pot or similar. When preparing food for babies, NEVER add any salt or sugar.

Frozen food will usually last for three to six months in a freezer kept at the required temperature. If you are putting fresh food that has just been blended into the fridge, it is best to use this within forty-eight hours. It's a good idea to label containers with the date before placing them in the freezer. Ensure that you defrost any frozen food carefully before heating it. The safest way to do this is to leave it in the fridge overnight or pop it into the microwave on the defrost setting. Throw away anything left over after it has been reheated from being defrosted.

Once your babies get to the stage of eating finger foods it makes it easier for you and the rest of the family to eat with them and in that way, they will get an idea of how it's done. It may not work out that the whole family can eat together on a daily basis, but it's definitely worth trying as often as possible. You will all come to enjoy this special time and hopefully you won't mind about the mess too much! An adult must always be with babies when they're eating.

You may find that your babies don't always like the same foods. While you are feeding them from the same bowl, you will want to make things as easy as possible for yourself so it is worth going with what you know they both like. Once they start feeding themselves, it is easier to offer them slightly different foods, but you will want to try and avoid preparing more than one dish for each meal.

Government guidelines on weaning babies can be found at www.eatwell.gov.uk under the Ages and Stages link for babies. If your babies were premature, you might find the booklet on weaning produced by Bliss, the premature baby charity, helpful. You can download it from their website at www.bliss.org.uk.

On the Move

Each new stage with your babies makes you aware of just how fast they develop and learn. Like little sponges, they are soaking up everything around them and it's worth taking the time to stop and watch them every now and then. Before you know it, they'll be crawling and if they are your first children, you will suddenly understand how many changes need to be made in your home. You won't be able to pop them down and take your eyes off them for a minute unless you're absolutely sure they are in a safe place. You may need to fix stair gates to stop them trying to negotiate the stairs. Stair gates can be used to block off one room which is totally child-friendly helps. Babies will be interested in anything at their level so all small or breakable items need to be hidden away and covers inserted into any electric sockets. You will find that at times one child will go off in one direction while the other sets off in the opposite so it's best to try to create a safe play area for them, where you know they won't come to any harm.

Mothers often comment on how they notice when they have twins or more that the babies seem to encourage each other that little bit more. Even at a young age they seem to feel they have the support of their twin, which gives them licence to be rather too adventurous sometimes. Also, at this age if one child tries to do something which you then tell them not to, there's a very good chance that the other will immediately try to do it, too!

❛Once they could crawl our daughters would constantly make a beeline for the bookcase: they'd pull all the books out and strew them all over the floor. To begin with, we tried wedging the books in so they were harder to pull out, but in the end we had to remove all the books from the bottom shelf.❜

Going Out

Getting out and about can be a major challenge with little ones. Sometimes it will take ages to get everyone ready and you almost wonder if it's worth the effort. Believe me, it is! It's good for all of you to have a change of scene and also something to look forward to, if it all seems to be getting too much at home. Make it easier for yourself by being as organised as you can. Aim to keep everything you need for going out in one place so it's easy to find. It might be worth getting into a routine of just checking where everything is and that you have what you're going to need. Try and do this whenever

you have a quiet moment when they're both asleep. Once you've done this a few times, hopefully it'll become a habit.

Going out for a walk with your babies in their pram or buggy gives you a chance to get some fresh air, a bit of exercise as well as a change of scene which always makes you feel better afterwards. Very often the movement will lull your children off to sleep, too. When you're out with your babies, you're more likely to meet other mothers. You might suggest getting together with another mum for a walk from time to time and could even get to treat yourselves to a cup of coffee or tea!

Going out with a double buggy does attract more attention and you will find that people stop and chat to you and want to ask all about your twins/triplets. It may not always be convenient but you'll find yourself feeling rather special and proud to show off your babies.

‛ *Getting out and about when they were tiny was very hard and we didn't do it much. Their first car seats were hardly used, but when I had a nanny we took them out most afternoons in the buggy together (I had my daughter too, who wasn't even two years old at that point).* ’

‛ *I was walking home from the park with my six-month-old identical twin daughters in their buggy as a group of Japanese tourists were walking towards us. They asked whether they could take photos of them and next thing we knew, we were surrounded by a load of cameras clicking away. The girls were most perplexed! I found it all rather amusing but you wouldn't want that happening to you every day.* ’

There are times when people will stop and ask what it's like to have twins. All too often you get the somewhat tactless 'rather you than me' or similar type of comment and if you're feeling a bit sensitive, this can seem rather hurtful but you have to remind yourself that you are the lucky one who has been blessed with these two, three (or more) gorgeous children. You will find it amusing to learn how ignorant some people are about twins and another question that is regularly asked is 'Are they identical?' when they are obviously a boy and a girl! Most of the time people are extremely complimentary and you should enjoy the praise – you deserve it.

Travelling by Car

There are specific regulations regarding the type of car seat required for babies and small children and it is important that you look into this before buying them for your family. You can find this information at http://think.direct.gov.uk/index.html. Make sure your car seats are properly fitted – this will depend on the individual make so check with the manufacturer's instructions. Before buying car seats, make sure that your car will be able to accommodate two (or more) of that particular model.

Rear-facing car seats must never be fitted to the front passenger seat if there is an airbag there. Fact sheets on how to safely install car seats are available from the Royal Society for the Prevention of Accidents (www.rospa.com). They can also give information on where you can get car-seat safety checks done.

Before you set off on a long car journey, make sure you have drinks and snacks handy to give to your children. A few small toys and books are also a good idea to occupy them and as they get older, music or stories on CDs will keep them quiet and content. It's also a good idea to try and plan a long journey to coincide with their sleeping time as the movement of a car does generally seem to send young children off to sleep. Of course there are also in-car DVD screens that can be attached to the seat backs and many people with multiples won't even consider travelling on long car journeys without them!

It is rare for babies to get car sick. If they do, you may want to plan ahead before taking a long journey by car. Pick a time when they haven't just been fed or when they are most likely to sleep and make sure they are not over-dressed.

'When young I found that the boys would sleep in the car within minutes of pulling away. When a little older, I found it best to take plenty of soft, easy-to-eat foods. And when a little older and still now for long journeys, having a few cheap little toys wrapped up would hold their interest, as well as singing and car games.'

Travelling on Public Transport

You can now take buggies on buses that are fitted with space for wheelchairs and buggies and this has made a big difference to parents of multiples. You no longer have to take your babies out of their buggy in order to fold it up before boarding the bus – something you just wouldn't be able to manage on your own with two or more little ones. This does mean that more parents travel with their babies on public buses and there may be times when you have to wait for the next bus because the first one to arrive already has a wheelchair passenger or a couple of buggies on board. It's a good idea to check with the driver first as generally you board the bus from the larger rear doors. Give yourself plenty of time when travelling in this way and when possible, avoid the rush hour. If you are in a hurry, try and travel with another adult who can help you take the babies out of their buggy, if necessary.

Trains and the London Underground may have more space for buggies, but you still have the problem of negotiating endless stairs or escalators. You will need to plan a trip of this nature well ahead and ideally have another adult with you to help. More stations are trying to improve access and this is usually indicated on the relevant websites. If you don't have someone to help you, try and contact the stations you will be travelling to and from in advance to check whether they will have a member of staff on hand who could help you. However, if they don't offer this service there is a good chance that a helpful passer-by will give you a hand although you may have to wait a bit.

Travelling by Plane

As well as being a busy time, flying during the school holidays and at weekends will naturally be more expensive. Before making an airline booking when travelling with twins or more, you should check with the individual airlines as to their policy regarding travelling with infants and small children. In most cases, babies up to the age of six months must travel on an adult's lap with the use of a special seatbelt attachment. So if you are travelling by plane with twins, triplets or more, you will have to have the same number of adults as babies. In some cases, particularly on long-haul flights, the airlines recommend you travel in the bulkhead seats where carrycots can be placed, but you will need to book these well in advance. Children aged between six months and three years can travel in an airline-approved forward-facing car seat (which you provide), but this will involve you having to pay for an extra seat on the plane for them. Once your child is two, you have to purchase a seat for them anyway and, particularly in the case of longer flights, you may find it is worth the extra money to get a bit more space for your children, even when they are under two.

You may not always be able to sit together on the plane as certain aircrafts are equipped with one child's oxygen mask per row. In addition to this, if you're using car seats, some airlines insist these can only be placed beside a window. It is advisable to pack individual carry-on bags for each child so that if you can't sit together, each adult can have baby things easily to hand. Again, it is best to check in advance with the airline as to exactly what you are allowed to bring onto the plane by way of food and drink for your babies. You will also want to have a change of clothes for them (and for yourselves in case of accidents!) and it's worth including a few carrier bags or similar to store any wet things.

Buggies can often be taken right up to the plane and are checked in as you board. This ensures your buggy will be there as you leave the plane but it's best to check with the airline first as they don't all have this policy. Try and travel with the lightest buggy you can. Some parents of twins have found that it is actually preferable to travel with two lightweight single buggies rather than taking a double one. They are easier to pack away and much simpler to manoeuvre. You could borrow from friends if you don't already have them.

Give yourselves plenty of time to check in. Everything always takes much longer with children and if you have more than one, this will definitely be the case – they often present unexpected surprises just at the wrong moment! Avoid having too many separate bags. If you've packed separate bags to take on the plane, you may find it helpful to put them into one larger bag for carrying purposes so you can then take them out once you're on board.

To ease your babies' discomfort during take-off and landing have something they can suck on. If you're breastfeeding, this is an option otherwise offer a dummy or bottle to ease the pain of the pressure they feel in their ears. If you can time feeding your babies so that they are hungry on take off and touch down, so much the better. When packing toys, you might find it best to take two of the same one to avoid any conflicts and make your trip as stress free as possible. Avoid taking any special toys that can't be replaced if lost and don't bring anything with small pieces that could disappear under your seat!

Ideally try and travel during off-peak times. Where possible, avoid flying during school holidays or at weekends and look at booking non-stop or direct flights if you can, however, you may feel that an overnight flight would suit you better as there is more chance that your babies will sleep then.

Travelling by Ferry

Another option to consider when travelling abroad with twins or more is to drive and take the ferry. This gives you the advantage of being able to carry all the extra paraphernalia that goes with small children in your car and you get the bonus of the adventure a ferry trip can provide. It's probably best to start off with a short ferry crossing to see how this works for you.

‹We didn't want to feel that having twins meant that we were no longer going to be able to enjoy travelling. My sister came with us on our first trip abroad when they were still small babies and this made such a difference to us. Having someone they knew well was lovely for us and for them.›

Home's Best?

Of course, while your children are still small you may find it easier not to travel abroad, and there are plenty of places to visit without needing to go too far. Sometimes just being away from home for a few days with the whole family can make a nice change for everyone. You may even find holiday properties that offer discounts to families with multiples through Tamba.

Notes

Chapter 5
Pre-school

‘The best reassurance
is knowing that you're
not the only one going
through the whole
bringing up twins thing.’

Individuality

As your children grow older you will notice each developing their own character and individuality, this should be encouraged as much as possible. Always try to use their names and look at them directly when you're talking to them rather than just glancing in their general direction. Where possible, give each of them the opportunity to have one-to-one time with you so that they don't always rely on doing everything together. At this early stage help them get used to being apart as early as possible even if it's only for very short periods of time. You will find it interesting to see how differently they behave when they aren't together.

It's not easy but try not to constantly draw comparisons between them, in the same way that it is unhelpful to compare your children with other people's offspring. They all develop at their own pace and it is stressful for all if you constantly feel that they should be keeping up with each other all the time. Of course, it is interesting to note the different stages as they reach them, such as when they start crawling, when they get their first teeth, their first words. It will be doubly or trebly exciting for you when the first child reaches a new milestone as the other will follow shortly afterwards. Try not to expect them to achieve these stages at the same time – you don't want them to feel as if they're competing with each other or their peers.

Bear in mind that generally girls and boys develop at different stages so don't expect them to be at the same level all the time. In their early years, girls usually develop a bit quicker than boys but this may not always be the case. If your daughter has started doing something ahead of her twin brother she certainly deserves praise and recognition, but he mustn't feel left out because he hasn't got there yet. Be aware of this and make sure that he gets just as much praise for what he *is* doing. Naturally the same applies to same-sex twins where their development is not always equal: both deserve to get praise and encouragement.

If you've always dressed your children in the same clothes this might be a good time to start dressing them differently. If they are boy/girl twins, it will be a lot more straightforward but if they are the same sex and particularly if they're identical, this needs a bit more thought. For practical reasons you may find it simpler to pick similar outfits in different colours but once they are old enough, encourage them to start choosing their own clothes as this provides a good boost to their individuality. Boy/girl twins have the advantage of being more likely to be treated as individuals right from the start. This is less likely if they are the same sex and even more unlikely for identical twins. In both cases it will require a bit more effort from you to help them be seen as individuals in their own right. You may find that one or both show a preference for certain colours and if this is the case, it certainly helps others to identify them easily, particularly if they are identical twins.

‹One of our identical daughters always wanted to wear yellow and we went along with this as it helped friends and family to tell them apart when they first met them.›

Of course they may both decide that they prefer the same colour, but there are always different options – spots, checks, florals, plains – encourage them to develop their own taste in clothes. There may be days when they want to dress the same, but generally they will probably be happy to express their differences. Of course there is always the added bonus, if they are similar sizes, that they can share clothes and if they're happy to do so, why not? However, if they show an attachment to their own clothes, this should be respected, too.

Sharing

As with clothes, there will be some possessions for sharing and others that definitely belong to one or other twin. It is important that they understand the concept of sharing and respecting each other's property from an early age. At this stage, this will mainly relate to their toys. It is unnecessary to buy two or more of most things (and it becomes expensive, too!) and it is important for children to learn to share. This is an advantage that multiples will have before they start school because right from the beginning, they always have to share.

' We bought our twins a portable plastic seesaw and it turned out to be a huge hit. They could use it outside or inside, depending on the weather. They spent many happy times on it together and when their younger brother came along, there was even a seat in the middle for him.'

However, there will be certain things that you will have to buy for each twin and so you need to consider this carefully before embarking on expensive purchases. Toys such as tricycles or scooters can't be shared so easily as it's much more fun if each child has one to play with. There will always be the inevitable situation where they want to play with whatever the other is playing with. One way to get around this is to have a timer to hand and allow them to take turns for a pre-determined length of time. Quite often you will find that the one who was so desperate to take the toy from their sibling is no longer interested in it long before the timer goes off!

Children don't need expensive toys – often they are very happy to play with things that you already have in the home (as long as they're safe). Items such as plastic containers, yoghurt pots, saucepans, wooden spoons, etc. are always popular, and frequently, a child will find the packaging of a new toy a lot more entertaining than the toy itself! Some children's libraries and Twins' Clubs lend toys, or you might try swapping certain toys with friends to provide a bit of variety. Tidying up toys at the end of the day can be made more fun by turning this task into a bit of a game. Small children often enjoy putting things into containers so you can make a game of this and get them to help you. If it looks like you're enjoying it, the likelihood is they will, too. Suggest timing them to see who puts their toys away first if they like a bit of a competition.

Toys that involve multiple components such as wooden train sets, building blocks or similar can be pricey but they last longer and can easily be shared by all your children. They also have the advantage that the more children you have, the larger and more interesting the sets can become if you encourage family and friends to add to the collection each birthday or Christmas.

Presents

If you know that family and friends will be giving your multiples presents, do encourage them to always give individual presents and cards. Half the fun is opening your very own specially wrapped gift – if you have to share this with your twin, some of the surprise is lost. There is often the temptation to give them one large present to share; there may be times when this is appropriate, but in general individual, smaller presents are more personal and exciting.

Parties

When your children are young they will probably be happy to share a birthday party and this could be the case when they get older too. However, you may find that they would much prefer to have their own individual parties. When they're sharing a party, try and give each one their own birthday cake. If you're not into making elaborate cakes (or just don't have the time), an inexpensive shop-bought cake will do – it's the fun of blowing out your own candles that's important to them!

Teamwork

As your children grow older so they will become more active and inquisitive. Each stage involves you having to rethink how to adapt your home accordingly. Once they begin to pull themselves up onto furniture and cruise around it you will become aware of just how much more they can reach. Once they are walking and learning to climb up onto furniture, more hazards will present themselves to you each day. There is no doubt that multiples can be more adventurous (and a danger to themselves) when working as a team – they do seem to encourage each other to do things that single children at the same age are less likely to attempt.

‘Our twins were always climbing onto any furniture they could and we'd find that together they'd worked out how to get onto the table after climbing on the chairs. For their safety and our peace of mind we had to lie all the chairs down on the floor – visitors were always rather surprised at the picture this presented when they first entered our home!’

Of course not all multiples will influence each other in this way, but it is as well to be aware of the possibility – that way you can be prepared. There will also come a time when your children start climbing out of their cots and this is good indication that it's time to move them into beds. This could mean that peaceful mornings will be lost temporarily until they understand that you don't particularly want 5 a.m. visits! You may feel that this is also the time to give each their own rooms – if your home has the space. If they are sharing a room, try and organise it so that each child has a little space that's theirs.

Safety at Home

Because your children are now on the move there will be certain safety measures you must take. If you have stairs, consider getting a stair gate and make sure that it is strong enough to support the weight of two or more toddlers leaning on it at the same time. Certain cupboards and drawers, particularly those in the kitchen and bathroom, must have safety locks fitted on them. You might want to keep one kitchen cupboard without a lock on it so that they can play with a few safe items – children are often very happy playing with wooden spoons, pots and pans or plastic crockery. It's a good idea to get doorstoppers, which will prevent them from shutting each other's fingers in the door and unused electrical sockets should be made safe by plugging socket covers into them. Teach them what is safe and what is not from an early age. This will need to be reinforced regularly. You mustn't rely on them understanding everything, but it is definitely worth persevering.

As your children become mobile, you won't have the luxury of popping them down for a minute and knowing they'll still be there when you come back so you will need to be extra-aware of where they are and what they are up to. If you have to leave the room to answer the door or attend to something elsewhere, it is best to create a safe space for them to be in, where you know they are not going to get hurt. You may find that a playpen (or even *two* playpens if you have the space) serves this purpose but do make sure if you are leaving them in one together that there is nothing they could harm themselves or each other with – wooden bricks and similar hard toys are probably not ideal for them to play with when in a confined space together.

As they get older, they will probably be happy playing with each other for longer periods of time and at around three years old, their play will possibly be a bit more structured. You should still keep an eye on what they're up to, though – it's amazing how quickly they can get up to mischief!

Unsocial Behaviour

Temper Tantrums

Tantrums will happen and particularly when your children are around the age of two (which explains the phrase 'the terrible twos'). Children are absorbing and learning so much at this stage in their lives and there will be times when it all gets too much for them – they are not able to understand a situation and this is upsetting and frustrating for them. They could be tired, bored, hungry, confused, or just wanting some attention and because their communication skills are not properly developed, the only way they know how to express themselves when they feel like this is by crying, shouting and generally making a scene. It's all part of growing up.

You may be able to work out what sets them off and if possible, avoid this happening by distracting them or dealing with it in advance. If you notice their tantrums happen at a particular time of day, it might be best not to plan to take them on a challenging outing at that time.

Each child has their own personality and you may need to adopt different methods to deal with individual tantrums. It could be that they set each other off – or one may look at the other as if they would never behave in that way! If they do set each other off, see if there's a way you can separate them until they have calmed down. It's hard, but you must try not to overreact and become stressed by their outbursts. Where possible, find a way of distracting without giving them too much attention. There are times when just changing the environment, is enough to distract them from their tantrum. Sometimes a hug is all that's needed, but this might just make it worse – you will soon work out what your children respond to best.

Biting

With twins, triplets and other multiples there is more chance that they will go through a phase of biting each other. Some single children try this out on others they play with in the playground or at playgroups. Yours are more likely to try it on each other! This doesn't make it more acceptable, but again it is something you need to be prepared for in case it should happen. It is something children do to each other and it causes a reaction so they try it again without really understanding that it hurts; sometimes it is done out of frustration or anger if they are both going for the same toy. You have to make them realise that this is not an acceptable form of behaviour and you are not happy with them when they do it.

❝ Mine have never bitten each other but a close friend's twins did. She found that getting each child to apologise and hugging and kissing was the best way forward.❞

If a toy is involved, it might be a good idea to remove it and bring it out again once things have calmed down. What you don't want to do is give the biter all the attention because often that's one of the reasons why they do it in the first place. As much as possible they should be spoken to gently but firmly and told they must not bite; also your attention should be focused on the one who has been bitten. Hopefully when the biter sees they are not getting the attention they'd hoped for – and in fact their sibling is – they will soon get the message that it's not worth the effort.

Fighting

This will happen – it's another element to growing up and a child's way of learning more about conflict, however, it can be upsetting for when it goes too far. There are differences between playfighting and the real thing and you will soon be able to tell them apart and react accordingly. Also, there will be times when you can just let them get on with it because it's all part of a game but when you sense that it's going too far, you must step in and distract your children before they hurt each other. Hopefully they will soon learn when to stop themselves but this may take time.

Boy twins particularly seem to need to fight as part of their playtime. They will playfight with their friends and with siblings and so are very likely to fight with each other.

Toys can often be the cause of disagreement between children and this may be when you need to intervene and suggest they take it in turns with the toy in question if they are not able to play with it together. Now would be the ideal situation to use a timer to keep it fair for all. Otherwise one child can play with the toy and the other can play with you for a bit and then you can swap round. If you can see an argument about to erupt you can prevent it by distraction but of course you can't be on the lookout all the time and they do need to learn to share and play together happily. It may be that there are times when one of your children needs to have their own space for a while; this should be encouraged, too.

Discipline

It's a good idea to talk this through with your partner first and then your children's carers so that you are all in agreement about what approach to take. This makes it a lot more straightforward for everyone as it can be confusing for children if they are getting different responses and no consistent guidelines to follow. Once you have established the rules of behaviour you must try and stick to them as much as possible – you want them to be clear as to what is acceptable and what is not.

At the same time you need to be aware that your children may behave in different ways: just because one has been naughty this does not mean that both need to be told off. You should look at the child who has behaved badly and make sure you use their name while you are explaining what they have done wrong.

If you are feeling daunted by the implementation of discipline, it is worth chatting to other parents to see what ideas they have and talking things over with your partner. There are parenting classes that many find very helpful, much literature is available and there are even TV programmes on the subject. You can't be expected to know it all right from the beginning and parenting is definitely not all plain sailing – when you've got twins or more there will be additional challenges for you.

As parents we're all guilty of saying 'no' to our children without really thinking it through first. Sometimes 'No!' seems to be the simplest response but it can be frustrating for them to be constantly greeted by a negative response. Of course there are situations where 'No!' is the only option but try to think it through first and see if there could be another solution.

Friendships

With twins or more you will find that they can be very happy in each other's company and play together for long periods of time, particularly as they get older. There will be times when this suits you, as you are able to get on with things at home without too much interruption. It's great to have these moments but also equally important that they should develop other friendships too. If you can encourage them to make friends through meeting other children in the playground or at playgroups this will be a good starting point for them before they start going to school. It is also a good way for you to meet other mums and dads with children of a similar age who live in your area.

If there are other children they enjoy playing with, you might suggest one invites a friend round to play while you organise it so that your other child goes round to another friend's. Try not to expect that both should always be invited out at the same time – other parents might find it a daunting prospect to invite two or more children to play with their child and will feel happier knowing they can invite one at a time. It's good for your children to have the opportunity to interact with others without their twin always being present. To begin with, if just one is invited out, it is natural that the other might feel left out. Try and pre-empt this by planning something special for the one at home. You could take them on a little outing with you, get a friend round to play with them or they might have some special one-to-one time with you and hopefully there will be a chance for them to go and play at a friend's another time.

Twins' Clubs

Another option may be Twins' Clubs. The advantage of going to a local Twins' Club is having the chance to share experiences with parents of multiples. Sometimes you can feel a bit left out at a regular mother and toddler group as most parents there will just have one child in their care. With two or more young children to look out for you don't seem to get much opportunity to relax and socialise! It's worth trying to visit a Twins' Club from time to time.

'The best reassurance is knowing that you're not the only one going through the whole bringing up twins thing and I've found my local Twins' Club a real help.'

Speech and Language

It has been noted that sometimes twins can take a bit longer to develop their speech than singletons. There are certain elements to being a twin that can affect their speech development. If they were born prematurely this should be taken into account. Also, twins usually don't get as much one-to-one time with an adult as a singleton might get and when they are with an adult, they usually have to share the attention.

Sometimes one twin does all the talking and the other twin is happy for them to do this. If this is the case with your twins, make sure you always encourage the quieter one to have their say, too. Let the talkative one know that they should each have a turn. Otherwise try and find a quiet time when you can be on your own with the one who isn't talking as much and encourage them to find their own voice.

People say that twins sometimes have their own language and this is reinforced by the fact that they spend a lot of time communicating with each other and therefore pick up each other's mistakes. They don't need to correct themselves as they understand each other so their 'own language' lasts longer than it would with a single child who will soon pick up the correct words from hearing others around them talking.

'The strong bond that unites most twins was very apparent early on: their likes and dislikes seemed to have been very similar, they played together very happily and often seemed to have developed their own special language for these play sessions.'

When twins are learning to talk they often don't get the chance to try their new skills out for long because chances are they will be interrupted by their sibling. You should be aware if this is something that happens on a regular basis and get them to understand that they should wait until the one speaking has finished before they join in. This is where treating your children as individuals becomes so important. You will help their language skills enormously if you can make it a priority to give them individual attention as often as possible. Grandparents can be a great help here, so encourage them to get involved.

If there is too much background noise when babies are learning to speak, it is hard for them to distinguish speech from everything else. It is important that they should have quiet time, preferably on a one-to-one basis so they can focus properly on the adult talking to them. If you feel they are not progressing well, it is worth having your child/children checked early. A good rule of thumb to follow is that they should be able to:

- Show an interest in people talking to them within the first few months
- Babble by twelve months
- Form single words by two years and be able to understand simple instructions
- Create early sentences by two and a half years
- Speak intelligibly by four years
- Use correct forms of grammar by five years

There is a feeling among some health professionals that delayed speech is expected in twins but if you are in any way concerned, insist on being referred to a speech and language therapist.

Potty Training

It may seem like a daunting task to potty train two or more children at the same time but it's normally not as tricky as you think – it might just be somewhat messier! There is no definite time by which a child should be potty trained (and indeed this varies from child to child), but you may find that they start showing signs of being ready for it between the ages of two and three years. Some take to it quickly while others are just not ready. One indication is that their nappy is dry when they wake in the morning.

As multiple-birth babies are often born prematurely you may find that yours are not ready as early as children born to term. Just because your children were born on the same day and even if they are identical, this doesn't mean they will be ready at the same time. If one is ready and the other isn't, do get started with the one who is keen to try rather than making them wait. Sometimes this can be to your advantage because by the time you've trained one child, the other will be ready and will have learnt what it's all about from their twin. This could make it a quicker process for you. However, this is not always the case. It's best to adopt a relaxed approach and not try to rush children into becoming potty trained, even if other people 'helpfully' suggest you should.

‘ Potty training was a breeze – my daughter was done in twenty-four weeks when she was three years old and her twin brother was done in a week when three-and-a-half (and dry at night at the same time). ’

There are various ways that you can tell when your child is ready for potty training. They may start taking their nappy off themselves or insist that it's changed as soon as it becomes wet or dirty. Also, they may be able to hold on for a while before needing to go to the toilet or prefer to go off by themselves whenever they are filling their nappy. It is a good idea to wait until they show that they are ready to be out of nappies before you embark on this task – it will take a lot longer if they're not prepared for it.

Once they have become used to the potty, they may want to start using the toilet. Encourage this if they are big enough to get up and sit on the toilet seat – they will probably need the help of a step to begin with for this (and also for washing their hands afterwards).

Potty Training Tips

- An ideal time to start potty training is when the weather gets warmer so that your children aren't wearing so many layers. If you have a garden at home, let them have time outside with nothing on (or at least they can be bare bottomed) so they get used to the sensations involved.

- It's a good idea to take them with you when buying their potties and get them to choose which ones they like. If they have been part of the decision they will feel much more involved and excited at the prospect of embarking on this new challenge. You will need to buy at least one potty per child – don't expect them to share! If your house is on more than one level you will probably find it easier to have one potty per child per floor to begin with rather than having to whisk them up and down the stairs depending on where the potties are.

- It is not a good idea to start potty training when there are other big events going on in your children's lives. If you are about to move house, starting nursery, or if you are having another baby, it may be better to postpone the event until things are more settled.

- Explain to your children what the toilet is for – and you may find it easier to let them observe you or older children using it. Teach them that the potty is their toilet and keep one nearby. There are a couple of different ways you can approach potty training. You can start by getting them to feel comfortable just sitting on it for a short time without their nappy on (they could be watching television, looking at a book or listening to you reading them a story while sitting on it) but remind them from time to time what it's for. Bowel movements often happen twenty minutes after eating breakfast so this might be a good time to try and get them to sit on the potty.

- Another approach is when you begin keeping the children's nappies off for an hour or so and gradually increase the time they are nappy-free. When they show signs of needing to go – they may start to wriggle a lot or hold their crotch – get them onto the potty as quickly as you can! This is when it's practical to have potties nearby … and make sure you have two to hand as the chances are they will both want to go at the same time.

- Give your children plenty of praise when they use the potty, even if nothing is produced, and try hard not to tell them off if they've had an accident. Accidents will happen in the early days and if a child becomes anxious because he thinks he's been naughty this will not help him to feel comfortable about the whole process. It all needs to be made as relaxing and normal as possible. If one or both of your children become ill during this time you may well find they need to go back into nappies for a bit.

- Sometimes children prefer not to be in the public eye when using their potties and may not even want their twin or other siblings to be with them. Try to be sensitive if this is the case and find a quieter place to keep their potties.

- Take them shopping with you to buy their own pants, too. They will enjoy this and it makes them feel excited about the stage they are at. You may find that your children are encouraged to use the potty when rewarded, either with a star chart or similar system.

- You will need to take two potties with you when you are out and about so it is worth getting some that are fairly compact in size. During the first few days while they are getting the hang of it all you may find it easier to stay nearer to home – or just to go out for shorter periods of time. Once they have settled into being out of nappies, take a bag with several changes of clothes when you go out as there will be times when they have accidents. The more prepared you are, the easier it will be for all of you.

Getting your children to stay dry at night doesn't usually happen until quite a bit later and there could be a difference in the time when each twin is able to sleep through the night without a nappy on. This can be a bit tricky because if one is sleeping without a nappy, the other may well want to do the same! You can let them try it out because sometimes after waking up in a wet bed they manage to control themselves within a few days, but this is not always the case. Some children sleep more heavily, drink more before bedtime or are just not quite ready even if they believe they are. It may be worth persuading them to keep their nappies on at night for a bit longer. Don't expect both children to be ready at the same stage – they will progress at their own pace. Waterproof mattress covers are invaluable if you haven't already got them.

We thought we'd cracked it with our daughters when they were two-and-a-half but then our son was born and "accidents" kept happening!

If one or both of your children do not seem ready to be potty trained, there is no point in forcing it. The more you pressure them, the more likely they will be to refuse. Give it a rest and try again after a few weeks. Try to be relaxed about the whole process yourself. If, however, you are concerned that there is more to it than them not being ready, it might be worth consulting your GP for advice, particularly if your children are over the age of three and have been trying to use the potty for at least six months without success.

Notes

Chapter 6
Other Siblings

'I feel very fortunate
that I had help with the
babies which gave me time
to spend with my older
child – it made all
the difference.'

Not that you have much choice in the matter but it's hard to say whether it's an advantage or disadvantage to already have children when your twins arrive. On the one hand, you have been through the experience of having small children to look after and it can be less stressful knowing there is an end to the various 'difficult' stages you can go through with growing babies. However, if you have other children to look after in addition to the new babies and you don't have any help, there is not going to be much time for you to sit down and catch your breath! It may also be that you had planned this pregnancy to complete your family and suddenly you're faced with the prospect of two or more newcomers to your brood. It can certainly be a challenging prospect for some and if you are feeling overwhelmed by it all, rest assured you're not the only one.

'My daughter was just a year old when we discovered I was pregnant again. I don't think we had expected it to happen quite so quickly and then we learnt twins were on the way. I have to admit I was terrified – I really didn't think I would be able to cope.'

Your Older Child

If you have an older child (or children) they will naturally be affected by a new arrival in the family – and two or more babies could present an even greater challenge for them to deal with. This will be the case particularly if you have an only child, who will be used to having you all to themselves and suddenly must share you with two or more babies, who will need a lot of help and attention to begin with. Having been the focus of all your attention – and all who come to visit – they will suddenly find themselves in a very different position and may find this hard to understand.

During this time, you will have to be sensitive to the needs of your older child as well as those of your babies and where possible, give your older child some time with you on their own. You might like to consider buying special presents that the twins can 'give' their older sibling when they are born. Also, encourage your older child to choose a couple of presents for the twins so that he/she feels more involved.

The evenings or nap times might offer an appropriate moment to spend with your older child (or children). They could even be allowed to stay up a bit later at bedtime to indicate that they are now growing up and in this way you can have some special time with them on their own. Take the opportunity to have a chat and listen to what they want to say. If they go to school, they may want to tell you about their day – try and give them a few minutes when they have your full attention.

It seems that boys frequently find it harder to deal with the arrival of new siblings. This could be because little girls still find ways of being centre of attention – they are more likely to want to copy what their mother does and will therefore be more interested in helping with the babies. Boys may show their feelings in a physical way without really understanding their behaviour. This could manifest itself in general bad behaviour to get more attention.

Depending on their age you can start to prepare older siblings in advance for the arrival of two or more new family members. However, it is probably best not to tell them too early as young children have a hard time understanding the concept of time and will only get confused. They will probably start asking questions when it becomes noticeable that you are pregnant – try to answer their questions as honestly as you can. If you are able to visit another family with young twins, this might help your older child to understand the concept of two small babies. Your health visitor or local Twins' Club may be able to put you in touch with a family with twins in your area. If this isn't possible, there are children's books that cover the subject of the arrival of twins into the family. You should explain that the babies are going to be very small and won't be able to do much apart from feed and sleep for some time so they don't expect to get instant playmates.

Where possible, try not to let your older child see you are experiencing any kind of discomfort during pregnancy as they may resent the babies for this. If they are already at school or going to a childminder, this will make things a bit easier for you and if they are about to start at school or nursery, it is a good idea to get them properly settled before the births. If time doesn't permit to get them established, then it might be wiser to consider waiting until after the babies are born – you should allow at least three months for this. They will find it hard enough to have to share you with the little ones, but to then be separated from you at the same time could be too demanding.

If they are already happily settled at school or nursery, you may find that they suddenly become clingy and upset at the thought of being left, but the chances are they will soon settle back easily. The same applies to potty training. Only attempt it before the babies are born if you have plenty of time to see it through. If not, there's no harm in waiting until some time after the babies are born. It does mean that there will be more nappies for you to change, but that might be easier than dealing with lots of accidents! The best thing is to try and stick to their routine as much as possible because they will certainly be affected by all the changes about to come their way.

You will also want to make sure there is someone they know well who they can be left with when you go into hospital, bearing in mind you could be there for several days, if not longer. Organise it so that they can come and visit you and the babies in hospital so they can share in the excitement. Again it is best not to let them know you are in too much discomfort as they could find this upsetting and it will reflect on the babies. While staying in hospital, try to phone your older child from time to time to let them know you're thinking about them. If you are in hospital for more than two or three days, it is likely that they will be very clingy and attention seeking on your return home. This will be hard as you will have your hands full with the new babies, but if you are able to acknowledge their need for reassurance and give them some extra comfort and encouragement, things will more than likely settle back into place more easily. At the same time you should keep to the routine and family rules they are used to so that they feel secure and loved.

It's quite common for older siblings to revert to infantile behaviour following the arrival of a new baby and the same applies if they have two or more siblings to get used to. They may want to drink from a bottle, or wear nappies again. Be prepared for some sort of reaction and try to give your older child as much attention as you can. Fathers or other family members can help by giving them some special one-to-one time. If you have friends or family visiting, encourage them to concentrate on your older child rather than spending too much time focusing on the babies. Alternatively, they could take the babies off your hands for a bit to allow you some time with your older child.

Feeding is probably the time when your older child is more likely to get frustrated – you have your hands full and are not able to react instantly to their demands. If they are still taking a nap during the day, try to arrange it so that this coincides with a feeding time for your twins. Alternatively, this could be an opportunity to introduce a special toy that you know will keep your older child entertained. It might be an idea to keep a box of toys, which is brought out when the babies need to be fed. Every so often, you could add new things to the box. A favourite TV programme or DVD could provide the necessary distraction at another feeding time. When you have finished feeding the babies, try to give your older child a bit of special time with you and praise them for their patience and good behaviour.

In some cases parents have been pleasantly surprised that their child has not reacted as badly as they had expected, suggesting this could be because the child saw that the babies were not getting much individual attention.

When you're out and about with two or more babies you will get a lot more attention and people will often stop you in the street to take a peek at them. If your babies are identical, there is likely to be even more focus on them. This can lead to your older child feeling left out. Where possible, include them in any conversation and draw attention to them, too. Otherwise, try and find times when you can go out together without the little ones.

If your older child is still at the stage where they get tired when you're out for any length of time, you will need to look into the best arrangement for transporting them. It is possible to buy buggies for three, four or more but you may feel that this is not practical from a cost or a size point of view. A lot of children are happy to stand on a buggy board, which can be attached to a double buggy, and there are some buggy boards that come with a seat attachment too. It could be that your older child feels resentful of their younger siblings because they are no longer able to sit in the buggy as they used to. While the babies are still small enough, you might want to consider carrying one in a sling so that your older child can sit in the buggy if you are out for a long period of time. Given the chance to sit in the buggy they well decide they would prefer to walk, but if the option isn't presented, they could feel put out and demand to sit in the buggy. Have a baby sling to hand just in case.

Tips for Dealing with Older Children's Jealousies

- Encourage them to have a friend round. If they are still quite young, it might be a good idea to suggest that the friend's parent comes too as you will probably need the extra help in looking after them. At least this way your older child won't feel they are missing out on things they are used to doing and resent the babies as a result.

- Include them in what you do with the little ones and make them feel important. If appropriate, ask them to help so they feel useful but don't put too much pressure on them to help all the time and be more grown up than they really are – they may not be ready for this and could feel overwhelmed. There will be times when you feel that they should know better and understand that you have your hands full and be more cooperative. They probably do understand, but at the same time they see you devoting so much time and attention to the little ones and they will soon realise that they can get your attention by doing something they shouldn't. This can create a pattern of misbehaviour and is best dealt with as soon as possible rather than letting it become a habit.

- Where possible, try to put the babies down so that you can devote some attention to your older child. If that's not possible, distraction can often be a good remedy and certainly better than getting angry – find something else to keep their attention.

- Praise and encouragement work so much better than negative remarks and if a child feels they are being good and it is being acknowledged, they are likely to react in a positive way.

Having two or more crawling babies interested in what you're playing with can be worrying for an older child who is protective of their special toys and games. You need to be aware of this and organise it so that they have a safe space where they can keep their belongings from being damaged or removed. If they have their own bedroom, a stair gate could be used to stop the little ones from invading at an inappropriate time. Alternatively, sit your older child up at the table with their toys, games or drawings out of reach of little fingers. You might find that a playpen comes in handy – either to pop the twins in once they are crawling or walking, or to pop your older child in with their toys. A playpen can also be a useful place to put your babies before they are mobile so that they are safe from the poking fingers of their older sibling! It is a good idea to try and devise games where they can all be included from time to time.

As they grow older it can sometimes feel as if the twins are getting together and ganging up against their brother or sister. They can come across as a dominant force but this may also work in a different way, where one of the twins and the other sibling form a strong bond.

‘I find that at this stage, with my older daughter aged five and the twins aged three, they don't play that well as a threesome but any combination of two and they can play really nicely together.’

When the time comes to place younger twins in school you may want to consider whether it is better for their older sibling not to be at the same school, particularly if they are quite close in age. Your older child may resent the extra attention the twins will undoubtedly get. This is more likely to happen if your twins are identical. If they are in different classes (and sometimes even if they are in the same class), non-identical same sex or boy/girl twins are not always recognised as twins.

Younger Siblings

If you have twins, triplets or more first, they will already have had to share you and will not feel the same jealousy at the arrival of a new sibling. You will have also gone through all the different early stages with your multiples and having a singleton will feel a lot easier. Of course, this all depends on the age difference between them – if your multiples are still quite young, having another baby may not be straightforward although the younger children will certainly get used to having less attention right from the start. One way to avoid difficulties is to carry the new baby in a sling as much as possible so that he benefits from being close to you while you still have both hands free for your older children.

Your baby will accept being a sibling of twins or more as that will be what she has known from the beginning and it may not be until she is older that she becomes aware that multiples attract more attention. He may not get all your attention but the chances are, he will attract a lot of interest from his multiple siblings. Babies are always fascinated by older children and are sometimes quite happy to be left in a bouncy chair where they can get a good view of what their siblings are up to. If there are two or more to watch, this could keep them distracted long enough for you to have a quick cup of tea and a chance to sit down for a few minutes! When your older children are still quite young it is not a good idea to leave them alone with a new baby, but do encourage them to become involved when you are around.

We felt it would be good to get our twins potty trained before the arrival of the new baby and thought we had cracked it. However, after his arrival they were forever having accidents – usually just when I'd sat down to feed him! I sometimes wondered if it was their way of getting my attention.

One advantage in having older twins and then a baby is that the twins are more likely to play together when you are busy with the baby. However, they will also be inclined to encourage each other to get up to mischief when they know your attention is elsewhere!

‘Having older twin sisters did sometimes seem to weigh quite heavily on their younger brother who came along two years later. One older sister can be tiresome for a lad, two is something of an imposition but with some inevitable friction at times, the family co-existence has worked out very amicably. They have developed a very real and deep affection for each other.’

‘Because the girls were such good friends together, with many shared activities and an "item", it was probably quite overwhelming for their younger brother. I think it was good that he went to a different school and made his own way without having to keep up.’

Chapter 7
Starting School

'Out of the three of us,
I think I was the one who
was the most anxious.'

For everyone within the family, starting school is a big and important event. You and your partner will have your own feelings about it and of course, so too will your children, particularly if they are your firstborn – it's such a new experience for all of you. On the one hand, you will probably feel ready to have a bit more time to yourself (if you haven't already experienced this by going back to work), but you may also question whether everyone is ready for the next stage. It is a big step and should therefore be treated as such.

This is probably the first long-term commitment you will make for your children and it is best to be well prepared. Apart from anything else, you want to make sure that you have made the right choice and your children will be happy and motivated. After all, they will be spending a large part of each day at school for many years to come. If necessary, changes can always be made but these may be unsettling for everyone concerned and if they can be avoided with a bit of forward planning, you will all benefit.

‘My daughters went into separate classes from reception on. For one this was absolutely no problem but the other took a little while to settle in. Out of the three of us, I think I was the one who was most anxious!’

One advantage that twins or more have over singletons when beginning their education, if they are attending the same school, is the reassurance of having someone they know well starting at the same time. Faced with a new environment and unfamiliar faces, it helps to have a friend close by. In fact, twins and higher multiples are often more distressed at being parted from one another than being separated from their mother. Their status as being part of a twin, triplet or higher multiple is likely to be as important to them as their age and gender and it is important to remember this. However, twins or more are already used to sharing their playthings, they expect to have to wait to get adult attention and are accustomed to having to take turns, so they often adapt more easily to a school environment than some singletons. As they get older, they will have the benefit of helping each other with revision and can give invaluable encouragement, too.

Together or Apart?

The main questions to ask when choosing schools:

- Are they going to attend the same or different schools?
- Which school (or schools)?
- If they are going to the same school, should they be kept in the same class or would it be best to separate them?

With triplets, the situation can become even more complicated:

‘We had a dilemma on our hands as to whether to send our two sons and one daughter to a school where they could all be in different classes or to send them to a one-class intake school, which had a better reputation. We decided to send them to the smaller school, which worked very well for the first three years but in Year 3, the boys had some behavioural issues which we didn't understand at first; there was also much conflict between them. The problem with being in the same class is that the children compared themselves to each other. One of the boys found learning very easy and was very bright, the other, although bright and eloquent, was slightly dyslexic and found this extremely frustrating, and this resulted in negative competitiveness.

‘We therefore decided to move them to a different school with a two-class intake. This way, the boys could be in different classes, with one of them sharing with my daughter. This was an agonising decision. Changing schools is not a decision to be taken lightly and did cause upset, in particular for my daughter. However, it was the right thing to do and all three children really flourished in their new school and their relationship with each other improved remarkably. Life was so much more harmonious and they all got along so much better.'

As your children get older, situations can change and it is worth being aware of this and prepared to be flexible, if necessary. It helps if the school can be flexible too.

School Policy

With twins, triplets or more there are additional issues to consider when applying for school places. You may want to keep your children in the same class or you might feel it is important that they should be separated. Whatever your views, it is important to check whether the local authority has a particular policy involving school entry for multiples. Currently 20 per cent of families are told that the school has its own policy when it comes to multiple-birth children and they are not open to discussion about it. Ideally, if you are sending your children to the same school, you want to find an establishment that is 'twin-friendly', where they are prepared to recognise the particular needs of twins while at the same time treat them as individuals. It is helpful if the school is willing to listen to your views on whether they should be in the same class or not. After all, you and your partner are the ones who know your children best and you'll have a pretty good idea of what works for them.

'When we sent our boy/girl twins to nursery we were told it was their policy to always separate twins. We felt this was appropriate for our two but looking back, I do wonder what would have happened if we had wanted them to be together.'

Some local authorities have admissions advisors who are independent from the admissions team. Their job is to help parents in their choice of school. If your area has an admissions advisor it's probably worth consulting them as they will be able to offer practical help and suggestions. Local authorities should have multiple-birth children included in the admission procedures, but approximately 50 per cent don't (it is best to check with your local authority about this). If you are keen for your children to attend the same school, you do need to highlight the fact that they are multiples on their application forms. There may not be an obvious place to indicate this so do check with your local authority before submitting the forms. It is also important to be aware of application deadline dates as they can vary from borough to borough. This information can be found on the relevant websites.

Be aware of the catchment area of each school you're looking at: if you are outside, or very much on the boundary, for a particular school, think carefully whether it is worth applying for places as you may be raising your children's hopes (as well as your own) too high.

If your local primary school only offers a one-class entry and you feel that your children would benefit more from being apart, consider sending them to different schools. This then brings up the question of location – how easy will it be for you to get to two or more schools each morning? As well as this, you need to think about other issues such as whether both school stipulate wearing a uniform? Are the school timetables similar? If your children hope to take part in any activities outside school, will they both be able to do the ones they want? Do they each have friends starting at the schools you have chosen as this may make a difference?

Each year approximately 100 families find that their twins are placed in different schools when they have particularly requested they be placed together. The sibling policy does not apply as twins would be entering the school in the same year and to benefit from the sibling policy, you have to have a child already in the school. Tamba have always been highly involved in the school entry process for twins and higher multiples and recently highlighted this and other problems that many families with twins or more have encountered through articles in the press. They have also campaigned to the government for greater recognition of the problems faced by some families with multiples when going through the school application process. If you feel your children have not been considered fairly when applying for a school place, it is possible to appeal. This is also an area in which Tamba can offer help and support. Appeals are generally heard from January through to July (and sometimes as late as August) and can be quite stressful.

If you are considering sending your children to private schools you will find their admissions policy and procedure on their website. It is a good idea to study them well in advance as application dates can vary. Alternatively, call the school to request a copy of the prospectus. It may be that your children are required to sit an entrance test before being accepted. Pre-prep (pre-preparatory) schools generally take pupils from ages four to seven years, while prep (preparatory) schools have pupils from eight to eleven and even thirteen. This varies from school to school, so check with the school website in the first instance.

Same Class?

If your children are placed in the same class or if there is only one class, it is possible to request that they be placed on different tables. It is very important that their teachers should be able to tell your children apart and treat them as individuals.

‘Whilst they are there together, they do play separately and the key workers have now learnt to recognise the differences between them and thankfully are able to tell them apart most of the time anyway.’

In the case of identical twins you can help their teachers to identify them. This tends to be more straightforward with girls as they can wear their hair differently, or indeed have it cut in contrasting styles to make it simpler to tell them apart. If you have identical boys, consider encouraging one to have his hair cut quite a bit shorter than the other – it does make a difference. Wearing name badges or, if it's possible within the uniform requirements, wearing different colours can ease identification for teachers. Some children may not be happy to wear name badges if they are the only ones doing it. Otherwise you could discreetly point out to your children's class teacher any distinguishing physical or behavioural differences. It is important that they are able to tell your children apart as quickly as possible.

‘ I found it interesting that my identical daughters' friends at school were able to tell them apart right from the beginning – but it took their teachers a lot longer!’

For parents worried about the decision of same class vs different class. Tamba has a questionnaire on its website that you can go through with the school to help with your decisions. It's a good idea to check with the school just how flexible it is and whether it might be possible to change classes, should the need arise. In some schools classes are mixed up as they go along, but if this is not the case you may want to establish whether you will be able to move one or both of your children if you do not feel that keeping them either together or apart is working. Ideally you should be able to assess the situation on a yearly basis with their teachers.

‘ They're in the same class – no choice as there's only one class. Next year, when there is a choice, I will separate them into two classes to allow them their independence as one twin tends to be more dominant.’

If children are kept in the same class you may find that some teachers tend to compare them, which can be particularly unhelpful.

During parents' evenings it is important to organise separate sessions with the teachers for each child so that the teacher's full attention is focused on one child at a time. If your children attend the parents' evening with you, it is important that they attend their slots separately too. Once again there is the need to highlight the importance of focusing on your children as individuals.

Different Classes

With twins in different classes, you will be more aware of the differences in teaching methods used by the teachers than parents with one child. If your children are going to be in separate classes, you may want to find out from the school whether you are likely to encounter these difficulties. It could be that one teacher may be keener to get their pupils reading earlier while another wants to focus on other skills first. Does one teacher tend to give a lot more homework than another? If you are aware of the differences beforehand you can be prepared as your children are bound to make comparisons.

Learning Together

Main reasons for keeping your children together at school:

- Your local school has only one class per year.
- Your children have never been separated before and you feel that this is not the right time to do so. This is particularly relevant if there are any major upheavals going on in their lives such as bereavement, divorce or the birth of a new sibling.
- They don't want to be separated and have expressed this strongly. It is not a good idea to force your children to be apart but you can

always encourage the school to get them to do certain activities separately.

- Your twins were at a pre-school together and you felt that this worked out particularly well.

Learning Apart

Some of the main reasons for separating your multiples at school are:

- The children themselves have expressed a wish to be apart.
- They are very different in their academic abilities.
- One may be overprotective of the other (more prevalent in boy/girl twins).
- They tend to distract each other on a regular basis.
- Together, they become very disruptive.
- They are extremely competitive with each other.
- Both try to work at the same level which may involve one attempting to keep up all the time or the other working less hard to compensate.

‘At nursery we started the boys with two sessions together and one separate each, but unfortunately neither child was happy to be without the other. The nursery did all they could do to help each child settle but the leaving them there apart was very difficult for the boys – they were not 'getting anything out of it. So we changed and put them in all three sessions together and they were much happier.’

‘Our five-year-old boy/girl twins are in separate classes at school and we definitely feel this was the right decision to have made. At this stage our daughter is way ahead of her brother academically and he would be much more aware of this if they were in the same class.’

Premature Babies

As twins are often born prematurely another question that often arises is whether those born in July and August (and whose due date would have been in the following school year) should be kept back either by a term or a year as you may feel they are not mature enough for school just yet. It is as if they are being forced to attend a year too early and they may struggle to keep up, which is not an ideal way to start their education. It's important to check whether, if they are kept back a year for primary school, they will also be kept back a year for secondary school. Some secondary schools insist pupils are admitted by their date of birth alone and will not take prematurity into consideration.

The charity Bliss is dedicated to helping families with children born prematurely. They are currently campaigning for schools to make their admissions policy more flexible when dealing with children who have been born before their due date, particularly those born in late summer and whose due date would make them a whole school year younger. In most cases, children who are born early adapt to school life without any problems but there are a few who might not be ready to start their education at the allotted time. They may have certain developmental delays and would benefit from starting school up to a year later.

Is One Twin Dominant?

Sometimes there is clearly a dominant child within a set of multiples who always takes the lead, some twins may alternate between being the dominant one and in some cases there may not be a dominant one at all. If one of your children is usually dominant at home, don't be surprised if the role is unexpectedly reversed at school as this does happen, particularly if they are in separate classes: the one who is usually more dependent then has the space to find his feet on his own and gain in confidence.

Getting Ready for School

If your children have already been to some form of pre-school, whether on a part-time or full-time basis, this will undoubtedly help when it comes to starting at full-time school. If not, it is a good idea to prepare them in advance. Talk to them about the school they will be attending and give them an idea of what to expect on an average day. Some schools organise 'taster' sessions towards the end of the summer term before the new intake of pupils is due to start (check with the school website). This gives your children a chance to get a feel for the school and to meet some of their future classmates.

If they can't already dress themselves or put on their own shoes, help them to achieve these basic tasks before they go to school. Make it easier by not choosing clothes with lots of buttons or shoes with laces. If they have a school uniform, encourage them to get used to putting it on beforehand and if your children are identical, think of ways to make their uniforms slightly different to help the teachers to identify them.

The more prepared they are, the easier it will be for you too. By getting themselves ready in the morning you can avoid the mad dash. It is a good idea to get yourselves into the right routine a few days before school starts so that you all feel ready for the big step. You could have a practice run to work out how long the journey takes and what you all need to do before leaving. Talk to your children about school lunches and what to expect. If either or both children are particularly fussy eaters, it may be possible for them to take a packed lunch to school. Encourage them to choose their own lunch boxes and find out what they'd like to take for lunch (within reason, of course!).

When they come home you may find that they are particularly hungry or tired and with multiples, it is smart to be prepared as the last thing you want is to have two or more grumpy children to deal with. Take some healthy snacks, such as fresh fruit or a packet of raisins, when you go to pick them up to avoid a bad case of irritable children.

They may want to tell you all about their day at school and if possible, give each child a bit of individual time to tell their story. Alternate so that each one has a chance to go first.

If you sense either of your children is unhappy at school it is vital to try and sort out the problem as early as possible. Talk to them and see if they can shed any light on what is wrong. It is also important to talk to their teacher/s from the beginning – you really don't want the problem to escalate.

'The local school has a one-class entry so our triplets were in the same class. I was worried that they might always be perceived as a threesome and wanted to make it clear that they were individuals too. I wrote a letter to all the parents who had children in the same class explaining that they mustn't feel obliged to invite all three to parties or to play – it was totally acceptable to just invite one. I feel this definitely helped, and my children have always had their own friends, as well as getting on well with each other.'

The ideal situation for multiple-birth children at school is where they show they are making good progress and are developing well as individuals. At the same time they are enjoying their friendships with other children as well as their twin/triplets.

Chapter 8
Secondary School

'Our girls really came into their own at secondary school. They were in separate classes and formed some very strong friendships but I was still aware that their main friendship was with each other.'

When it comes to choosing a secondary school, local authorities have different approaches. Some allow you to choose three schools, others up to six and it's quite likely their policies will change over the years. In view of this, do make sure you have all the necessary information to familiarise yourself with your local authority's policies. At this age your children are likely to want to have a say, too. This is a time when they will have opinions of their own on which school they would like to attend, if they want to go to the same one and whether they want to be in the same class. Ensure you have the chance to talk these important decisions over with them and where possible, visit the schools together. It is essential that they take an active part in deciding which secondary schools they want to apply to.

If you are thinking of educating your children privately, you will need to contact your chosen schools directly to obtain information on their admissions criteria. This may be available online or the schools will send you their prospectuses. Application procedures and deadlines vary, so it is important that you familiarise yourself with these in good time. It may be that your children are required to sit an entrance test and some schools still expect certain results from the Common Entrance exam, which is taken either at the age of eleven or thirteen. Some private secondary schools (particularly mixed ones and girls only) start at eleven in line with the state system. The more traditional boys' secondary schools begin at thirteen.

Decisions, Decisions

It may be that your children have been together through primary school, either in the same or separate classes, but now feel they would like to go to separate secondary schools. On the other hand, they may want to stay together at secondary school, having attended primary school together or having been at separate primary schools, they may want to team up and go to the same secondary school. Conversely, they may be very happy at separate primary schools and want to continue with this arrangement into secondary school. With lots of possibilities to consider it is worth spending some time with them, both together and individually, to make sure that you are all clear as to what their preferences are. In some cases multiples may each make a decision based on what they think the other wants and it is important for you to emphasise to them that they should make their own choices.

‘Our daughters were at the same primary school – in separate classes – and were keen to have the same arrangement when they transferred to secondary school. Fortunately this worked out for them and they both settled into their new secondary school happily.’

‘*The primary school our triplets went to had a two-form entry so two had to share, which was a difficult choice for us to have to make. They recently moved on to secondary school, where they are all in different classes and independent of each other.*’

When choosing secondary schools for your children you will also want to think about how easy it is going to be for them to get to school. At this stage they will probably be keen for a bit more independence, and if it is easy for them to make their own way to school, this will certainly help.

Entrance Exams

You want to be realistic with your school choices. Some secondary schools have additional entry requirements such as entrance exams. If your children's abilities are very different, do consider whether it is sensible to put both their names down to sit entrance exams for the same school/s when you know that one is likely to struggle to achieve the required grade. It may not be helpful to raise their expectations too high if it is likely one of them won't achieve the required results – they will only be disappointed if they don't get offered a place and their confidence will take a knock. It makes more sense to apply to schools that suit their individual abilities and if these are very different, it is probably best for them to apply to separate schools.

If your children are sitting exams for a selective placement or a scholarship to a particular school you do need to think carefully about how you will deal with the situation, should only one of them be successful in gaining a place. It is a good idea to be prepared for the day entrance results are announced – even when your children's abilities are very similar it is possible only one will be offered a place following the entrance exam. It is a good idea to be as positive as you can about all the schools you have applied for as it may happen that one of your children does not get offered a place of their first choice. You want them to feel confident that the school they're going to has just as much of your support as the first-choice establishment that their sibling has got into.

Appeals

If you are unhappy with the school (or schools) that your children have been offered and feel your applications have not been considered fairly, you can put in an appeal. As with primary school applications, Tamba has an honorary consultant who may be able to help you with secondary school appeals. Going through the process of appeals can be time-consuming and stressful, but it is definitely worth doing if you feel you have a good case. This is where Tamba can help.

School Policies

Once again, if your children are to go to the same school, you will have to decide whether to keep them in the same class or allocate them to separate classes. As with primary schools, some secondaries will say they already have a multiple policy in place in which case it is worth talking to them about this in advance. Ideally, you want to choose a school that is prepared to listen to your requests as well as those of your children (not all multiples have the same requirements). If you are finding it hard to decide what is best for your children, refer to the questionnaire on the Tamba website. If you still have problems making up your mind, Tamba can refer you to honorary consultants who may be able to offer their expertise and guidance.

Identical?

If your children are identical and it is decided that it is in their best interests to keep them in the same class, it really is a good idea to try and help their teachers to find ways in which they can identify them. By the time they reach secondary school age they may well have started to adopt their own styles, which will certainly help. However, do bear in mind that if they are wearing a school uniform it may not be all that easy to make them look different. If it is hard to tell your children apart, involve them in deciding what they might do to make it easier for their teachers to differentiate. At this age they are more likely to be cooperative if the decision is theirs rather than yours or something the school has decided on.

At their secondary school your children will have many more teachers than at primary school and because of this, each teacher will spend less time teaching them. This means that it could take longer for them to learn to distinguish between your children if they are identical.

Streaming/Setting

If you have opted to keep your children in the same class it is worth bearing in mind that secondary schools will often stream or set according to pupils' ability in certain subjects. This could mean that they will not always be together throughout the school day and you might want to make them aware of this possibility in advance especially if you already know they have very different abilities. You will also want to make your children aware of the streaming system if it has been decided that they should be in separate classes at the same school. If they are similarly able in certain subjects, they may find themselves in the same set. Some schools may have more than one class for each set, in which case they can still be separated but this may not always be the case.

Just because your children are multiples does not mean that they will always learn in the same way. They may have very different approaches to schoolwork and you should not expect them to study similarly. Equally, you want their teachers to realise that they may have very different individual needs and that it is unhelpful to be make constant comparisons.

Parents' Evenings

‘Secondary school was a lot harder because they were always scheduled on the same day and there were multiple teachers to see. At first I would go early and stay late but this meant that teachers were telling me things about one daughter while the other one was present. Depending on the content, this wasn't always appropriate.’

At secondary school parents' evenings it is likely your children will be required to attend with you. This makes it even more important to have separate slots for each child and to make sure that only the one you are discussing with the teacher is with you at that time. For twins, the ideal is to have two adults to attend each parents' evening and for triplets, three adults. This is where a grandparent or other family member may be happy to help out, if given sufficient notice. It is advisable to take a notebook with you so you can jot down important items discussed with each teacher and talk about them when you get home.

Special Needs

If one of your children has special needs the other may adopt the role of carer at school and this could become a burden to them. The child with special needs may become too dependent on their twin. Might it be better for them to go to different schools? This is a question you will need to ask yourself.

Growing Up

Secondary school entry is just around the time when your children reach puberty and so you need to be aware of the stresses that go with this. This is highlighted particularly with boy/girl twins whose rates of development are likely to be different, especially as girls generally reach puberty earlier. A boy twin may not have the same degree of maturity or confidence as his twin sister and could suddenly be regarded more as an annoying younger brother. In cases like this it might be advisable to place your children in separate classes so that they are not automatically compared.

If it is any comfort, it is rare to find that children are not happy with the school they are placed in once they have had the chance to settle in – even if at first they were disappointed with the choice.

With the move from primary to secondary school, you will notice that you won't have as much daily contact with the school as you may have had when your children were younger. They are more likely to be making their way to and from school without your help and as a result you may feel you are not so in touch with what they are up to. Make time for them to tell you individually about any particular events that they may want to share with you, encourage them to talk to you one at a time and ask them not to interrupt each other. If it's possible to give them a bit of one-to-one time, even better – this does not necessarily have to be every day but it is important to let them know that there will be times when they have your undivided attention.

Subject Choices

As your children progress through secondary school they will be asked to make subject choices for their GCSEs and A-Levels. When the time comes, it is a good idea to check with them their reasons for choosing particular subjects. It could be that they are following each other's choices because they don't have the confidence to take different subjects. On the other hand, they may feel they have to choose differently because they don't want to be seen to be doing the same thing. Find the time to chat with them individually about their subject choices so that you are all happy that they've made the right decisions and aren't feeling pressured by their twin or by anyone else. You want them to realise that it's perfectly acceptable to do either the same or different subjects so long as this is what they want to do. What is important is that each is choosing the subjects that she is most interested in and happiest to learn.

If your children have a particular path that they want to follow, it is important to ensure the subjects they choose are appropriate when the time comes for them to make further education or job applications. The school should be able to advise you on this matter.

‘When it came to the time to choose A-Level options our daughters chose a couple of the same subjects. This did mean that, having always been in separate classes throughout their schooling, they were in the same class for one of their A-Level subjects. They rather enjoyed having this opportunity to share a bit of class time together.’

Studying for Exams

All children have their own method of studying and they should be encouraged to follow their own style. When you have two or more teenagers studying for exams at the same time it is important that they should each be given the space and encouragement they need. Some children prefer to be on their own while others may want to be together. It is probably a good idea to ensure that they each have their own personal working space and if they want to study together from time to time, somewhere like the kitchen table can come in handy. You might like to suggest that they think ahead and work out a timetable, which could include some study time together if they are working on the same subject. It can be helpful revising alongside someone else but there will definitely be times when they need to work individually, too.

‘GCSEs seemed easy because they took a lot of similar subjects and were at a similar standard so they did a lot of revision together and that seemed to work well. However, when we got to A-Levels things were not so easy – the studying required more independent learning and this suited our son much more than our daughter.’

Exam Results

The day major exam results such as GCSEs or A-Levels come out is certainly an anxious one. It is important that your children should pick up their own results and they can then look at them with you or privately. If you have encouraged them in the past to have their own time to tell you their special news they will be used to this and will appreciate that this is when they need to give each other one-to-one time with you. You may find that their abilities are very different and this must be taken into account when the results are published. If they have achieved the grades that they were predicted they must be praised – even if their twin has done much better. It may be that one child does particularly well and the other unexpectedly hasn't achieved their predicted grades – this can be hard as you don't want to overdo the praise for the one who has done well, but at the same time they do deserve it.

⟨ When we got the results our son had done really well but our daughter hadn't, so we found ourselves waiting until she left the room before we could really celebrate with him. It was a very difficult time but we got through it. She then found a course that really suited her and her relationship with us and her brother is as strong as ever. ⟩

Further Education

When the time comes to consider whether your children want to continue with further education it is important to focus independently on each of them. It may be that they both want to apply to college or university once they have finished secondary school. If this is the case you will want to set aside sufficient time to be able to sit down with them individually to go through their various options.

As with subject choices, when they come to choose whether they want to apply to go on to college or university make sure they are choosing for themselves and not basing their decision on what their twin/triplet has already chosen. The choices they are making are important and could affect their whole lives – you want to be sure they are making them for the right reasons.

Notes

Chapter 9

The Teenage Years

'A single teenager can
be absolutely impossible
at times – there's no
way twins can be
much worse!'

Identity

Most teenagers feel the need to find a positive self-image and there are times when they question who they really are. With twins and other multiples, particularly if they are identical, this may be accentuated. They need to know who they are and should be encouraged to explore their own individuality from an early age.

'For many years now they have been totally individual and though they do have many qualities in common, they are complete personalities in their own right.'

Some teenage twins feel that it's important to keep their multiple status while others want the opposite. According to Ann Landers, well-known American agony aunt who is also a twin, an important motto for multiples is: 'The one thing that I can do better than anyone else is be myself'.

As your children become teenagers you might feel it is time to consider giving them their own space, if they haven't already got one. You may not have enough room at home to accommodate a separate bedroom for each but if space allows, it might be possible to divide their shared room in such a way that each feels they have their own area.

'When our daughters started at secondary school we felt the time had come to give them a room each but unfortunately our house wasn't big enough. Luckily the room they had always shared was big enough to put up a partition wall and this gave them their own space.'

If you are able to divide their bedroom, they can then assert their own individuality by choosing how they want to decorate their space and establishing their personal style.

Boy/Girl Twins

Girls tend to mature faster and in the case of boy/girl twins you may find that your daughter is no longer as keen to spend time with her brother – or at least not when her friends are around. He may suddenly seem a lot younger than her and this can be upsetting for him. Fathers play an important role in their son's upbringing at this stage and can help them grow in confidence by showing their approval and offering them one-to-one time. If your boy/girl twins have been at the same school up until now, you may feel this is the time for them to go to different schools.

There are all sorts of changes going on with your teenagers at this time, emotionally and physically. The physical ones are the easiest to spot: one of your twins might suddenly have a growth spurt, leaving the other one behind. If they are both boys, this can make a big difference. As boys grow at such different stages, it can be bad enough watching your classmates overtake you but if your own twin brother does the same, this can be quite hard to cope with – particularly if the difference is very noticeable. Likewise with girl/boy twins it is quite likely she will have a growth spurt first and overtake her brother. You must encourage him to understand that this is all quite normal and the chances are he will soon be overtaking his sister. All he has to do is look at older teenagers to see how boys tend to catch up in the end.

It's also a time when one or both of them may develop acne, start experimenting with their appearance – wanting to dye their hair, get piercings or tattoos or, particularly with girls, use more make-up. With all the physical changes taking place, they may also become prone to mood swings.

If you look at similarly aged teenagers, you are bound to notice some are maturer and more ready to take on a more independent role than others – just because they are twins, this doesn't mean that they will always be developing at the same rate. However, they may gain confidence from being together and if one is a little more hesitant, then the other might provide sufficient encouragement to give them the confidence they need.

Quite often girls show signs of wanting more independence earlier than their brothers. They may focus more on their friendships and are keen to be out doing things with friends.

‘Our triplets are now thirteen and our daughter loves to join her friends on the bus and go shopping locally. Her brothers are still very happy to stay at home and play.’

Puberty

Just because your children are multiples does not necessarily mean that they will reach puberty at the same time. Weight can play a role in deciding when your children start to experience the changes of sexual maturity. Girls are unlikely to reach puberty until their critical body weight is around 47kg (7½ stone) and with boys, the weight is 55kg (8 ½ stone). Identical twins are more likely to grow at the same rate and therefore have similar weights, so they may start puberty at around the same time but this is not always the case.

Twin girls may get their periods on the same day but equally there may be a gap of three to six months or even up to a year. Bearing in mind that girls get their periods anytime between the ages of ten and seventeen, it's not surprising that there should be a gap between twins. If there is a significant gap it may affect their relationship: the one who hasn't yet started her periods may feel that her sister is more grown up than she is. At this age, they are often very keen to be grown up and she may feel jealous and resentful as a result. On the other hand, the twin who has her periods might feel that life is moving faster than she wants it to and find herself wishing she could be more like her sister.

❛ *There was about nine months difference: one at twelve and one at thirteen. This actually corresponds in body size. The one who was born 1.5lb [0.6kg] heavier started puberty earlier. However, they were both club-level swimmers and had lots of muscle mass. This tends to delay puberty (you need a certain fat: muscle ratio for periods to start). Couldn't tell much difference early on with mood swings – similar patterns then and now!* ❜

It is a good idea to gently explain this when difference in maturation you're talking to the girls about puberty and what to expect when their periods start. After all, they won't be starting their periods at exactly the same time as all their friends.

The same applies to buying their first bra. You may find that one of your daughters develops sooner than the other. Fortunately, nowadays there are so many pretty bras available in all shapes and sizes that girls who really don't need to wear them have plenty of choice. If one of your daughters is less developed, she doesn't have to feel left out – if she wants to keep up with her sister, she can always go for one of the smaller sizes.

Becoming More Independent

You may find that your twins start to adopt their own style and choose to dress in a totally different way. Identical twins in particular might want to highlight their individuality. On the other hand, teenagers often want to look alike and even if they don't have a uniform at school, they all seem to end up wearing very similar clothes. Same sex twins, and girls in particular, have the advantage of having someone else's clothes to borrow – somehow the wardrobe of another is often more interesting than their own! Your twins will start wanting to be more independent of you and begin going out on their own with friends. If they are your first children you will find some reassurance in the fact that they may choose to go out together on their first 'solo' outings.

‘Living in London I was happier knowing that they were travelling on the Underground together when they went without me for the first time.’

There is definitely that 'safety in numbers' feeling with twins or more. Knowing they'll be watching out for each other will give you the confidence to let them have their independence. You may find that their relationship with each other becomes stronger at this point as they come to rely on each other in a more adult way. However, you cannot count on this being the case and it may be that as they get older they prefer to do things separately and don't always want to feel they have to stick together for safety's sake. Just because they are twins doesn't mean that they will want to do the same things, meet up with the same people or go to the same parties and you will have to make allowances for this.

As with other teenagers you can request they go out with friends rather than unaccompanied, particularly at first when they haven't the experience of travelling around on their own. You will certainly find that other parents will be experiencing the same concerns. It's a good idea to arm your teenagers with some safety advice before they start going out on their own. They should always let someone know where they're going and when they'll be back. Wherever possible, they should travel with friends and stick to routes and areas they know well. If they're not comfortable in a particular situation, they shouldn't be afraid to say so. The chances are they will already have mobile phones but if not, then consider getting phones for them.

'It's nice to know that I can contact them when they're out – mobiles have been a good investment.'

In the 1980s a survey was carried out on 600 adult twins and their parents with the help of the *Observer*, the *Daily Express* and *Woman* magazine and the results are discussed in Mary Rosambeau's book, *How Twins Grow Up*. One interesting finding was that in several cases, teenage twins seemed to take their frustrations and anger out on each other rather than their parents. Maybe this is a reward for the extra effort you've had to put in during the early years? Of course this is not always the case and there are bound to be some 'teenage moments' in your relationship with your twins. Rosambeau also observes that in some cases twins tend to rely more on each other during their teenage years, giving each other support against what they deem to be the unfair rules imposed on them by their parents: 'About half the twins in the survey had managed to establish their separate identities within the partnerships without this sort of conflict. Their growing apart had proceeded imperceptibly and for them the positive support of having a twin had come into its own'.

Even if your twins have separate friends they will reach an age when their social lives may coincide as they are mixing with a larger group of their own age. If you have boy/girl twins, they will be more used to having each other's friends around and this could be an advantage when it comes to the beginning of relationships. On the other hand, it could be that one becomes more protective of the other.

To some parents, the teen years can present challenging times and if you have to support two or more teenagers during this changing period it can double the stress. You are obviously keen to support both children equally, but at the same time you want to recognise their individual needs. There will be times when you will find that battling against two or more children over particular issues can be very tiring and you may feel it's almost easier to give in, but in fact teenagers appreciate having reasonable boundaries. There will be occasions when it all becomes rather overwhelming for them too and knowing you are there to provide them with guidance and support really helps.

You can also find yourself all too easily saying no to whatever request your teenagers make just because you've got into the habit of rejecting their proposals. Before answering, stop for a minute and think carefully as to whether their request is really so unreasonable. You may be surprised to discover there are times when you might agree to a request and then find they don't actually want to do it, but were almost 'testing the waters' to get a reaction.

Friendships

Twins often share friends, particularly as they go into their teenage years when they seem to accumulate new friends all the time. All you have to do is see how many 'friends' the average teenager has on Facebook to understand how important friendships are at this time in their life. They have been used to sharing throughout their lives and as part of a pair, twins may find it easier to form new friendships.

‘We did feel at times that their close bond might lead to an apartheid as far as making friends was concerned, but this was not the case – they have all through their lives readily made many very close friendships, which have endured.’

There can, however, be situations where multiples have been so close to one another that they find it hard to develop strong friendships with others. This could also be the case once they start to become involved in relationships with girlfriends or boyfriends. They may feel it is especially important to keep their strong bond with their twin/triplets going and the prospective girlfriend or boyfriend might find this hard to accommodate.

It's good for teenagers to know that their parents are there for them when needed but you must try not to get too involved in their friendships. At times they may have to learn the hard way about the vagaries of teenage friendships and relationships but it will certainly benefit them in the long run and if they have the added security of knowing their parents will always support them emotionally, this will be a huge bonus.

Chapter 10
Leaving Home

'Both have told me that
when they are apart and
haven't spoken for a few
days they have to contact
each other, even just
for an argument.'

It is likely that by the time they reach their teenage years your twins will have achieved a degree of separation from you and rely more on each other. However, they may not experience a long separation from each other until they leave home to start their further education.

‘When they were kids, they didn't really have autonomy. However, when they were teenagers, they had to stick together through some very difficult times. They drew strength from each other in a way that they didn't need when younger. This may be a close sibling thing but I would say it's intensified with twins.’

As one of the twins from Mary Rosambeau's survey in her book, *How Twins Grow Up*, commented, 'Any book on twins should cover the actual separation. From personal experience, this is one of the most traumatic times for a twin – really a typical word is grief'. It is not always this way but it is advisable that a parent should be aware of such a possibility. If your twins have never spent any time apart it may be particularly hard on one or both of them when the time comes to go their separate ways.

The family therapist Audrey Sandbank puts it most succinctly in her book, *Twins and the Family*: 'So the adolescent twin, like a caged bird with the door open, may sense his need for freedom but lack the will to fly out, afraid of facing the world alone. Every encouragement is needed to help the bird flutter free with the door left open so that the return is not barred'.

One result from the survey that Rosambeau notes is: 'It was significant that those who had found it difficult to separate when they were older had almost always shared a room'. Here again the argument for separating twins into their own bedrooms presents itself. It definitely helps if your children have been encouraged from as early an age as possible to develop independently and have not been made to do the same things all the time. If they have taken on different interests over the years, they will have had time to get used to being apart even if only for short periods – it all helps in the long run.

From a parental perspective it can often be a lot simpler to have them doing the same activities. A good example is when they are invited to go and stay with their grandparents and of course as a parent, you will see this as an opportunity to have some 'child-free' time together with your partner. However, if there can be occasions when the twins are sent to stay with their grandparents separately this can be a way to help them get used to being apart. It also presents you with a wonderful opportunity to have one-to-one time with the remaining twin while the other one is enjoying having their grandparents all to themselves. Make sure you are able to offer this arrangement to each twin. If you have triplets, this could still be arranged if you have two willing sets of grandparents but may involve considerably more planning!

Challenging Times

When your children reach adolescence you may start to feel rejected by them; see this as a form of preparation for the future. They are learning to go their own way and may not always want your help and advice as they did when they were smaller. The same could apply to the relationship between your twins. You may notice that they now seem to reject their 'twinness', they may have more arguments with each other and outbursts of anger and frustration. This could be a reflection of their fear of separating from each other and way of dealing with these new emotions. It's a natural way to react and it helps if you're aware of this and can be there to offer support but it's not a good idea to get too involved if you can help it. If you can be there for them both as impartially as possible, this will make a big difference to you too. Teenagers are known for their volatile emotions and can easily hate each other one moment and then love each other the next. This can be a bit of a rollercoaster ride for you but if you're prepared to be open-minded and not too judgemental, things should be easier for you.

'Both have told me that when they are apart and haven't spoken for a few days they have to contact the other one, even just for an argument, because they feel something missing.'

Of course there will always be situations where twins just do not want to be parted and you may need to work harder to help them enjoy time apart. There is no doubt that a special bond develops between the majority of sets of twins/triplets or more – most have spent all their lives together and know just how the other thinks and feels. By sharing so much, they offer each other such security and stability that they may come to rely on each other a little too heavily. Ideally, you want to encourage them to remain close friends while at the same time showing them the way to give each other the freedom they both need.

There are cases where one twin may want to go their own way, but the other is eager for them to stay together. This can often be the way with girl/boy twins, where the girl matures faster and is keen to start leading a more independent life. Her brother, on the other hand, may want to hang onto their childish games and the support they offer each other. This will be a time when both need extra help and understanding from you. It is quite possible that the one who wants more independence may feel guilty and therefore becomes angry and frustrated with their sibling. If you are able to talk to them both, individually and together, about what they are feeling and what is going on in their lives, they may be able to see things more clearly and understand why they are experiencing these emotions.

Quite often the first time for twins to separate is once they've finished school and are about to go away to study at college or university. If they have not had much opportunity to be apart from each other before this event you may find it takes them longer to settle into their new life than their fellow students. It might be worth suggesting they visit each other so that they can picture where they are when apart and they will also have a chance to meet each other's new friends. This can be easily followed up with modern technology.

❛We keep in touch with each other all the time through Facebook, Skype and texting. We were even able to compare the sizes of our rooms in hall with our webcams! Mine was a lot bigger!❜

Having always had someone else around to help when making decisions and to talk over important issues with, it can be especially hard for twins when they're off on their own. Of course there are always other friends but between twins there is often an understanding that comes with having been together all the time.

Sometimes they might expect rather too much of friends in this respect. Also, it may well be that they were unaware of the important role the other had in their life until they were apart. Twins are often each other's best friend without really expressing it in that way – they just don't feel the need to have a special friendship with anyone else because they already have each other. This is probably more the case with twins of the same sex and they may not form a strong friendship with anyone else until they go their separate ways.

❛My daughters never had "best" friends at school as they always had each other and shared a large group of very good friends, but when they went to university they both made "best" friends very quickly.❜

Coping with Departures

Having twins, triplets or more can make parents feel 'special'. If you are out as a family, particularly if your twins are identical, people will notice you and often stop to confirm you have multiples. If the subject comes up in general conversation, people are always interested to know more about what it's like to be the parent of multiples and at times, you can become the focus of attention. When your children leave home it is possible you may feel this 'loss' more. For a start, having two or more members of the family leave at the same time will have a practical impact – you have fewer people to feed, less washing to deal with, less general mess around the house and so there are some positive aspects to look forward to! However, at the same time there's less company around the house, fewer family members to chat to and a definite feeling of emptiness, which can take time to adjust to. You may not feel so needed and will also, quite rightly, feel your life has changed yet again.

It's a good idea to try and prepare yourself in advance for when this time comes so that you're not suddenly left feeling a bit lost and abandoned once your children have flown the coop. If you already have plenty of other interests, that's great because you'll now have more time to indulge yourself and enjoy them and if not, this may be a good time to think about finding new activities including some that you can share with your partner. You may have other children still at home in which case they are bound to keep you busy and now it will be their turn to get more of your attention.

‘When our twin daughters left home to go on their gap year our younger son had us all to himself for the first time. I realised that they had often taken over the conversations at mealtimes and now he was getting a chance to have his say.’

If your children have left home for reasons of further education then the chances are they will be home on a regular basis, particularly during holiday times. University and college terms seem to be even shorter than school terms and you will find that just as you are getting used to living in a quieter, less chaotic household they're back, loaded with washing. There may be weekends when just one comes home and you get to spend time with them on their own, which is always nice. There will be more times when they are both home and you will probably notice how quickly they click back together.

> ‘They both believe that they are physically bonded together and separation causes actual pain.’

It's always exciting to have them back home again, but it can also alter the balance of things at home when two or more members of the family who have been away for some time come back. You may find this particularly if you have other children still living at home; be aware of this and try not to focus all your attention on those returning home. Those still at home will have got used to perhaps getting a bit more of your time and may not be happy to relinquish this attention too readily. On the other hand, they may be delighted not to be the sole focus!

Notes

Chapter 11

From A Father's Viewpoint

'Looking back, twins
undoubtedly changed my
bank balance for the worse
but my life for the better.'

'Finding out that you're having twins is a bit like being hit with a huge tax demand and then realising later on that you've actually won the Lottery!'

You probably know the feeling when you've had a minor car accident – shaking and weak at the knees from the impact, you stand by the car viewing the damage but relieved no one was hurt. Well, that's the feeling you are likely to experience as you walk away from the scan when they first tell you that your partner is expecting twins. As your knees recover, you walk tall with a residual teenage angst about virility forever banished and a scientifically unsound view that you personally have achieved something special ... and then the fun starts.

During the pregnancy be as supportive as you can and attend the pre-natal classes with your partner. You should certainly go to all the scans as they are fascinating and by far the best evidence you'll get that something amazing is going on.

Getting the house ready is a key task as there will be no chance of DIY-ing and repairs during the first eighteen months of your twins' lives. If you have a car, you may need to change it for one with a bigger boot to hold a double buggy and other twosome equipment. Perhaps the most important task is to nurture your relationship with the future grandparents, with particular attention reserved for the mother-in-law – you will need as much credit as you can get in the coming months.

As the birth date approaches your partner's mobility is likely to become more and more limited so you will need to be especially attentive. Taking care of the shopping and helping with cleaning, cooking and other household chores as well as providing regular refreshments for the expectant mum are all part of your role. The babies are likely to arrive early so preparatory jobs around the house need to be finished early.

The Arrival

At the birth you must realise your role while essential to the whole process is little more than that of a walk-on extra on a film set. Your partner is the star of the show and there is likely to be a full production crew of trained professionals who have done this before (we had twelve people in the birthing room at the peak and they all seemed to be doing something useful and important).

Firstly, you are responsible for getting your partner to the maternity ward. Tempting though it might be to become an ad-hoc ambulance driver, this is probably not the best strategy for delivering your loved one in the calm and controlled manner that she deserves. On the other hand, it's also not the best occasion to fuss about the possibility of a parking ticket.

Once at the hospital you are your partner's assistant and moral supporter. There is no way that you can predict how the labour will proceed so it's advisable not to have a rigid birthing plan. Meanwhile, see yourself as a runner, on hand at your partner's every beck and call – you do not have to suffer the pain of labour so get ready to work in other ways. Be prepared for multiple, parallel and mutually inconsistent requests. Your tasks may include managing communications with the outside world, providing magazines and other small comforts, running out to stock up on the nappies that you forgot to buy in advance and even going over the optimal combination of names yet again.

While there will be times when you and your partner are equally overwhelmed by medical attention, there may be strange periods of calm when the nurses, doctors, mid-wives and anesthetists all seem to disappear to deal with other tasks. At this stage you need to be with your partner, encouraging and ready to go in search of support when the next phase kicks in. You may even be sent home to get some sleep if the whole process stops for long enough. After all, there's no point in everyone being exhausted.

The moment of delivery, or technically the *moments* as it's twins, is wonderful and weird in equal measure. Of course you need to be there but out of the way unless you are asked to get involved. I am sure it's different every time but our twins were delivered surprisingly quickly with little chance to fret about what was going on or whether it was going to be OK. Like all momentous occasions, I remember the event in fragmented snatches – here the first sight of the emerging baby reversing into the world, there a tiny cry, there a wave of relief as both were delivered with all the requisite parts intact. Most extraordinary of all was how small they were – easily supportable in one hand and yet each a new human being in her own right.

The immediate post-natal period is a strange time when the great deed is done but the complications may not be over. Your partner is exhausted, barely able to attend to one baby, but in this case there are two to consider. You hope both will be able to stay with their mother but this may not be the case. For us, 'Twin 2' had to go into the Neonatal Intensive Care Unit for thirty-six hours and so as the Father my main role was to sit with her, bond and give frequent progress reports. Fortunately everything went well: the tubes were soon removed and the new family unit was quickly re-united.

While all this is going on, your other role will be to manage the equivalent of a Downing Street press office in letting family, friends and colleagues know the good news. In this age of digital communications and on-line collaboration, I guess an essential task for the well-prepared partner is to have the message lists set up and the wireless laptop on hand. Except for close relatives and friends, texting is ideal as you don't have to deal with responses there and then. Don't forget your partner's work colleagues – they will be expecting news within hours and if they are good ones, there may be a bottle of champagne in it for you, too.

Post-birth photos are a tricky issue. You will certainly feel that your babies are, unlike all others, exceptionally beautiful within minutes of the birth but go cautiously with the digital camera. Well-wrapped babies in their mother's arms with little more than a button nose or tiny finger showing will draw the necessary cooing from the recipients and won't cause you retrospective embarrassment in later years.

Back Home

Once the babies are home and for several months afterwards, the father remains very much in a support role. Particularly if these are your first children, it is helpful to have someone on hand who has been through the whole baby process before as there is so much that you will have no idea about. This is where the earlier softening up of the mother-in-law can be particularly invaluable although you may have to work on smoothing out a few inevitable mother-daughter differences of opinion. It's a small price to pay for a lot of practical advice and moral support for your partner, though.

If you have the option, don't take all your paternity leave in the first couple of weeks after the birth. In general, there is greater support for your partner during the first few weeks than later on, so you can be at your most useful when the other relatives and medical helpers have moved on. The first three or four months seem to largely consist of an endless round of feeding, nappy changing and trying to coax the babies to sleep. In all likelihood, your partner will be exhausted and often stressed about whether she is doing the right thing. During this time she will need lots of reassurance and emotional support from you.

Breastfeeding two babies simultaneously is a feat and not something that is easily done unobtrusively in the corner of the room. There is not much you can do to help with the task itself so the important thing is to make sure that the conditions are as comfortable and convenient as possible. Expect the sitting room to be turned over to this activity as watching television is about the only thing your partner can really do while feeding the new arrivals.

If your partner is bottle feeding (and it is likely you will at least be topping up with a bottle), this is where you comes into your own. Several feeds a day, two mouths at a time, adds up to a lot of bottles, teats and tins of formula milk to be sterilised, mixed and made ready. It is the perfect activity to make you feel useful while your partner is doing the last feed of the day and allows you to go to bed in the knowledge that you are sharing the load.

It is tempting to feel that you must be awake and supporting your partner with the inevitable feeds in the middle of the night during the early months. Certainly you should be ready to help get the babies out of the cot and fetch the necessary breastfeeding accoutrements but beyond that you may as well turn over and go back to sleep as there is little point in both parties being exhausted, fractious and likely to snap at each other the next morning. Of course, if the babies are being bottle fed then there is no excuse for failing to share the full bliss of sleep deprivation!

On the positive side your twins will be entertaining and fascinating from day one so spending as much time as possible holding them, playing with them and just observing them is a joy not to be missed. As with any baby, the speed of development is incredible and with twins, there are extra little points of interest such as watching how they interact or, if they are identical, trying to work out which one is which. Indeed, this can be a uniquely difficult challenge. Coping strategies include looking for tiny telltale marks that give the game away, calling a name at random and seeing who responds and later, when the twins are old enough to cope with it, pretending that you are mixing them up deliberately as an amusing diversion.

While it is undoubtedly true that twins can be hard work during the first months, it is generally not as demanding as you think. A single first child will take up a lot of your time and twins take up even more – but you learn how to do things in parallel and perhaps not to worry quite so much about achieving absolute and unattainable perfection in all that you do as a new parent. The difficult times usually pass quite quickly and from about twelve months on, you start to get the payback as the twins learn to amuse themselves, to play entertainingly together and to communicate in ways only they can truly understand. From that moment on, I think twins actually require less intensive parental attention than a single child who relies on his parents for nearly all his social interaction in the early days.

Growing Up

As your twins become older, you will inevitably think about how you want to bring them up. Your behaviour and the way you relate to your children and to others will be an important influence on them. You can spend as much time as you like telling them what you believe they should do and how you think they should behave, but it is your behaviour that they will follow. They will detect, as perceptively as any adult, where your true values lie and in the long run, this is the only thing that you can really expect to pass on to them, so spend time with them, talk to them as equals from an early age and involve them in your everyday life as much as you can. In this way it's no different with twins than with any other child.

Where twins differ is that they have an additional critical

influence on how they grow up – and that is their twin sibling. The most useful insight that I have read about twins was the notion that they need to grow up developing both an individual and a joint identity. That is to say, they conceive of themselves both as an 'I' and as a 'we'. It's a concept that I doubt any non-twin will really understand but it still needs to be allowed for. This being the case, I think that it's not the role of either parent to promote the 'we' identity but rather to permit the conditions where this can evolve naturally between the twins themselves. In practical terms it means not indulging in twee parent-pleasing strategies such as dressing them identically but rather letting your twins choose freely what to wear, which items to monopolise and where to inter-change. It means letting them develop friendships in their own way and being willing to open up your home to lots of children, as two socially active kids may well mean double the number of visitors and sleepovers. Treat them fairly but not identically with favours, presents and sanctions too. And it also means never calling them 'the twins' to their face or in their absence.

As they grow older, encouraging a certain degree of separation will help them develop their independent identities, but I believe this should never be forced on them. Most schools seem to have an enlightened attitude towards twins, assigning them where possible to parallel classes and letting them develop separate interests. In the early stages particularly, this feels like a better solution than insisting on separate schools unless their educational requirements are markedly different. As they move into higher education, I think it is permissible to have a discussion with them about the pros and cons of going to separate institutions but the final decision needs to rest with your children without a feeling of undue parental pressure.

Spending time with each twin on their own can be surprisingly hard to do but it's well worth the effort, especially if as the father you are out of the house during much of the week. It's good for children to get the male perspective on things and you can introduce them to ideas and activities other than the ones they share with their mother. Constructing the opportunity around some form of treat or expedition creates an ideal environment, but it's the individual attention rather than the specific activity that really matters. This provides an opportunity for a different level of conversation and interaction with each child than is possible in the group setting – you will learn more about their feelings and hear observations and insights unlikely to be expressed in normal day-to-day activity and when the excursion is over, you will feel that you have established a closer bond and discovered an extra thing or two about the personality that is developing in front of your eyes.

Most of the ideas and views in this chapter could apply equally well to a single child as to twins. There is little qualitative difference in the things you need to do to be a supportive father regardless of the number of children you are dealing with and how close in time their birth dates might be. Ultimately all you can do is try and create the most favourable possible conditions for your children to grow up in – and what matters is their emotional, not their material surroundings. With twins you may have to work a little harder at first but sooner than you imagine, they will take a load off your shoulders in the way they support and entertain each other. When this happens you will have the immense privilege of watching joint and individual personalities emerge in a way which less than one in fifty parents can enjoy!

‘Looking back, twins undoubtedly changed my bank balance for the worst but my life for the better.’

Notes

Chapter 12
Grandparents

'I rarely asked my
mum to step in and help
out but when she did,
she was a godsend.'

When you first discover that you are expecting twins or more it is likely that the first people you tell will be your parents. Don't be surprised if their reaction is not quite what you expected:

‘My mother's reaction when I first told her we were expecting twins was that she had been told the same with each of her pregnancies so I wasn't to take it too seriously. I had to explain that I'd actually seen them both on the scan to make her realise that this *was* serious. In her case there were no scans – the doctor had thought they'd heard two heartbeats and advised her that she might be expecting twins.’

Your parents and parents-in-law may become very excited at the prospect of becoming grandparents to multiples and could well want to be more involved than if you were expecting just the one baby.

‘When we first heard that twins were expected there was perhaps an added excitement because there would be the bonus of a "family" at one go.’

Grandparents can offer help in many ways and sometimes slightly unexpectedly ...

‘The babies' early arrival presented immediate practical problems as our daughter's kitchen was being rebuilt to be ready for the forecast birth date. This was great for us, as once out of hospital they came to stay with us and we had two absolutely happy weeks helping to look after them all. We'll never forget bathing them in the kitchen sink before we had got around to procuring a baby bath.’

This can be a huge bonus to you and to the grandparents but it is worth thinking it all through in advance so that you are aware of how this new relationship will benefit everyone (the babies particularly) in the best possible way. If you're lucky and have parents who are young at heart and in good health they may be able to help in many practical ways. Having two or more babies, you will be aware of what a bonus an extra pair of hands can be. If that help comes from someone as close to you as a parent, you really can't ask for more.

You can be sure they will love their grandchildren unconditionally and be prepared to do almost anything for them. Generally, children have a special relationship with their grandparents – there is a recognisable bond that attaches them to each other that appears to come naturally. Children must sense something of their parents in their grandparents and this enables the seamless link to happen, particularly if they are in contact on a reasonably regular basis. If you are able to benefit from this special relationship, do make the most of it as it will certainly be extremely helpful as your children grow up.

If you have parents who are keen to help, live nearby and have some time (they may be retired when your babies are born), you could discuss whether they might be able to set aside one or two days a week to help you out, particularly in the early months after the birth. Even if they can only manage a few hours, this will be a big help to you. In the early weeks when you might feel a little trapped at home because you just seem to spend all your time feeding and cleaning up after your new babies, you will probably enjoy having a bit of company and someone around who you can ask to do the odd job without feeling you're being demanding.

If your parents or in-laws live further away and you have a spare room at home, you might consider asking them to come and stay with you from time to time – again to be on hand to help with whatever needs doing. They will probably be only too happy to be involved with their grandchildren from an early age. If they get to develop a good relationship with them right from the start, it will grow into something very rewarding for everyone. You benefit from having totally trustworthy childcare, your children enjoy getting to know their grandparents and hopefully your parents will find the whole experience a hugely rewarding one (even if it can be totally exhausting at times!).

If you already have other children, their grandparents can enjoy some special time with them while you're preoccupied with your little ones. Your older children will certainly enjoy being spoilt and given the extra attention that you may not always be able to lavish on them when your time and energy are in demand elsewhere. This will be a lot easier to organise if your children already know their grandparents well and feel happy being with them.

It is helpful to go through any particular points that you feel are important and not to presume that just because they are grandparents, they will know exactly how to deal with your children. There are certain guidelines to childcare that change over time and it is a good idea to bring grandparents up to date with these. Sleeping positions for babies is a case in point and it is important that they should be made aware of the current NHS advice that babies should be placed on their backs with their feet at the end of the cot or pram. Likewise if you have any particular wishes, talk these over with them. In the case of multiple-birth children, particularly with identical twins, you may want to try and make it as easy as possible for them to be able to recognise them as individuals. Speaking of her identical grandchildren, one grandmother comments:

‘In their early months and years I think we tended to think of them as an "item" and so their development was duplicated rather than individual. From about two years old, different characteristics began to be more noticeable.’

Encourage grandparents to use their names whenever speaking to their grandchildren and ask them not to call them 'the twins' when they're with them. You can help with this by not dressing your babies in the same clothes (or at least not too often) so that it is easier to tell them apart.

‘ With twins (as a grandparent) I think you should try straightaway to treat them individually, i.e. different presents and toys at Christmas and birthdays, different clothes and maybe outings.’

If your parents are not in a position to help on a regular basis, either because they live too far away or are not fit enough to manage, they may still want to contribute in other ways. Giving financial help can make a difference too. If your parents or in-laws have indicated that they would like to make a financial contribution, you might suggest that they help towards the cost of a maternity nurse when you first come home with your babies. Alternatively, they may be able to contribute towards the cost of either a home help or an au pair so that you can benefit from an extra pair of hands at home while your new family is demanding so much of your time. Talk this over with them to make sure they are happy with the way in which their gift is going to be used.

A Special Relationship

As your children grow older they will come to appreciate the special bond they have with their grandparents if they have been given the chance to see them on a regular basis. Likewise, for grandparents, having the opportunity to be involved in their grandchildren's development can be hugely rewarding.

‘Watching them growing up was such joy as they got on so well together.’

Your parents will enjoy seeing your children grow and will also be aware of any special bonds between them:

‘ One interesting twin feature we (as grandparents) have noticed over the years is their ability to share the telling of a story – intuitively one is able to take over the thread from the other without any dispute.’

Having grandparental involvement may be of great benefit to you, too. In some cases new mothers in particular find that their relationship with their own mother changes as a direct result of having children:

'I felt closer to my mum after my children arrived. They were obviously very comfortable with each other and I was grateful for the break. She didn't undermine me or comment negatively on my parenting skills. She realised that raising twins presented different challenges. It made us closer.'

There may also be times when you really appreciate having someone step in at short notice to help with your children and usually the first people you're likely to ask are your children's grandparents:

'I rarely asked my mum to step in and help but when I did, she was a godsend'

Grandparents often enjoy having their grandchildren to stay and you might like to suggest that they have them to stay on their own from time to time so that they can have the benefit of their grandchildren all to themselves – children do seem to behave better when their parents aren't around!

Children can benefit hugely from the time their grandparents have to devote to them. They may learn particular skills from them, hear wonderful stories or just enjoy the fact that someone is prepared to drop everything for the time they have together.

'My mother-in-law taught our children how to bake bread and this is something they really enjoy doing now. It's certainly not something I would have been able to teach them!'

You may not mind your children jumping on the sofas at home but this may not be appropriate at their grandparents' house. Generally, children learn quite quickly what is appropriate behaviour when they're with the older generation. Of course, this can work the other way and they may manage to convince their grandparents that their bedtime is a lot later than it really is. A quiet word in advance may be helpful.

It is important to remember that grandparents will not have the same level of energy they had when they were parents of young children. Remember this to avoid exploiting their naturally enthusiastic willingness to help. You will require their support for many years, so use it judiciously.

‘ *It is important from the start that grandchildren, twins or not, realise that Granny and Grandpa's rules and customs appertain in Granny and Grandpa's house!* ’

Grandparents Plus – 'The national charity which champions the vital role of grandparents and the wider family in children's lives' – has a very helpful website (www.grandparentsplus.org.uk) with a considerable amount of information on how grandparents can become involved in their grandchildren's lives and what a difference it makes when they do.

Finally, there is no doubt that a really important bond is formed between children and their grandparents and it's one that will stand them in good stead throughout their lives.

Notes

Resources

General Help and Advice

Tamba (Twins and Multiple Births Association) the largest UK organisation supporting multiple-birth families
2 The Willows
Gardner Road
Guildford
Surrey GU1 4PG
01483 304442
www.tamba.org.uk

Tamba Twinline 0800 138 0509
(a confidential listening service for families of twins and more – everyday 10 a.m. to 1 p.m. and 7 p.m. to 10 p.m.)

MBF (The Multiple Births Foundation)
Hammersmith House Level 4
Queen Charlotte's & Chelsea Hospital
Du Cane Road
London, W12 0HS
020 3313 3519
www.multiplebirths.org.uk

TEDS (Twins Early Development Study) One of the foremost ongoing twin studies of its kind in the world
www.teds.ac.uk

Twins' Clubs

Contact Tamba for details of your nearest Twins' Club

NCT (National Childbirth Trust)

Enquiries 0300 330 0770

Pregnancy and birth line 0300 330 0772

www.nct.org.uk

NHS has a very helpful and informative website

www.nhs.uk

NHS Direct for health advice and reassurance 24 hours a day, 365

days a year

0845 46 47

www.nhsdirect.nhs.uk

Maternity

AIMS (Association for Improvement in the Maternity Services)

Helpline 0300 365 0663

www.aims.org.uk

Maternity Action for help with maternity rights

020 7253 2288

www.maternityaction.org.uk

Department for Work and Pensions (DWP) provides information

on maternity leave and pay

www.dwp.gov.uk

Pregnancy Related

Tamba's '**The Healthy Multiple Pregnancy Guide**' can be downloaded from www.tamba.org.uk

BabyCentre a very informative pregnancy and parenting website www.babycentre.co.uk

APEC (Action on Pre-eclampsia)
Helpline 020 8427 4217
www.apec.org.uk

OC Support UK for information and support on obstetric cholestasis
Helpline 07538 585047 (10 a.m. to 1 p.m. Monday to Thursday)
         07939 871929 (7 p.m. to 9 p.m. Monday, Wednesday, Thursday)
www.ocsupport.org.uk

Twin to Twin Transfusion Syndrome
Tamba's '**Twin-to-Twin Transfusion Syndrome: A Guide for Parents**' can be downloaded from www.tamba.org.uk/TTTS

UK Twin to Twin Transfusion Syndrome Association
www.twin2twin.org

Doulas
Doula UK
0871 433 3103
www.doula.org.uk

British Doulas
020 7824 8209
www.britishdoulas.co.uk

Postnatal and Prematurity

Tamba's **'Multiple Births - A Parents' Guide to Neonatal Care'**
can be downloaded from www.tamba.org.uk

Bliss the premature baby charity
Freephone 0500 618 140
www.bliss.org.uk

Tamba's **'Postnatal Depression: A Guide for Mothers of
Multiples'** can be downloaded from www.tamba.org.uk

APNI (Association for Postnatal Illness)
Tel: 0207 386 0868
www.apni.org

Breastfeeding

The breastfeeding guide **'Feeding twins, triplets and more'** can
be downloaded from www.multiplebirths.org.uk

NCT Breastfeeding Line 0300 330 0771
www.nct.org.uk

Breastfeeding Network Supporterline 0300 100 0210
www.breastfeedingnetwork.org.uk

Association of Breastfeeding Mothers
Helpline 0844 412 2949
www.abm.me.uk

La Leche League
Helpline 0845 120 2918
www.laleche.org.uk

NHS
www.nhs.uk breastfeeding section

Ameda to buy or hire breast pumps
0845 009 1789
www.ameda.co.uk

Breastpumps
01538 399541
www.breastpumps.co.uk

Bottle Feeding

NHS
www.nhs.uk bottle feeding section

Podee Feeding System a hands-free bottle feeding system (please note babies must not be left on their own at all whilst bottle feeding)
07716 009850
www.podeestore.co.uk

Yoomi a bottle and warmer in one – at the touch of a button
0800 066 9950
www.yoomi.com

Crying Babies/Baby Massage

Cry-sis offers support for families with excessively crying, sleepless and demanding babies.
Helpline 08451 228 669
www.cry-sis.org.uk

International Association of Infant Massage
020 8989 9597
www.iaim.org.uk

Free Help at Home

Home-Start UK the UK's leading family support charity which places volunteers with families in need where children are aged under 5 – including multiple birth families.
0800 068 6368
www.home-start.org.uk

Cache contact them for your local college running Level 3 diploma courses in childcare and education as students are often keen to get experience by helping families with small children
0845 347 2123
www.cache.org.uk

Paid Help

National Childminding Association
0845 880 0044 or 0800 169 4486
www.ncma.org.uk

Daycare Trust the national childcare charity which provides information on a range of childcare options
Information line 0845 872 6251
www.daycaretrust.org.uk

Norland Nannies
01225 904030
www.norlandagency.co.uk

Children With Disabilities/ Medical Conditions

Contact a Family provides support, advice and information for families with children with a medical condition or disability.
Helpline 0808 808 3555 (9.30 a.m. to 5 p.m. Monday to Friday)
www.cafamily.org.uk
www.makingcontact.org to contact a family in a similar situation

One Parent Families

Gingerbread
www.gingerbread.org.uk

Lone Parent Helpline operated by Gingerbread and One Parent Families Scotland
0808 802 0925 England and Wales
0808 801 0323 Scotland
www.loneparenthelpline.org.uk

Parenting

Parentline the helpline for Family Lives which is a national charity providing help and support in all aspects of family life.
Helpline 0808 800 2222
www.familylives.org.uk

Mumsnet a website for parents and parents-to-be
www.mumsnet.com

Netmums an online parenting organisation that can link you up with other mums in your area
www.netmums.com

Equipment

Tambas' Pushchair, Pram and Buggy guide can be viewed online
If you join Tamba you will be eligible for discounts from a wide range of baby equipment suppliers
www.tamba.org.uk

Car seat fitting
http://think.direct.gov.uk/index.html

Royal Society for the Prevention of Accidents
www.rospa.com

Freecycle a useful source of items offered for free in your local area
www.freecycle.org

Education

Twins and Multiples Australian university-based website providing information on the educational needs of multiple-birth children

www.twinsandmultiples.org

Teenagers

Got a Teenager social networking and advice site for parents of teenagers – linked with Parentline

Parentlineplus 0808 800 2222

www.gotateenager.org.uk

Fathers

Home Dad UK a support group for stay-at-home dads

01938 810626

www.homedad.org.uk

Grandparents

Grandparents Plus champions the vital role grandparents can play

020 8981 8001

www.grandparentsplus.org.uk

Further Reading

Tamba have a number of booklets on multiple related topics that can be downloaded from their website www.tamba.org.uk

Cooper, Dr Carol. *Twins and Multiple Births: The Essential Parenting Guide from Pregnancy to Adulthood*, Vermillion, London, 2004

Mahony, Emma. *Double Trouble: Twins and How to Survive Them*, Thorsons, Wellingborough, 2003

Rosambeau, Mary. *How Twins Grow Up*, The Bodley Head Ltd., London, 1987

Sandbank, Audrey. *Twins and the Family: The Essential Guide to Bringing Up Twins*, Tamba, Guildford, Surrey, 1992

Notes

Index